discard.

Aaron Copland

Aaron Copland
His Life

by CATHERINE OWENS PEARE

illustrated by Mircea Vasiliu

HOLT, RINEHART AND WINSTON
New York   Chicago   San Francisco

Cover photograph by Alexander Courage.
Frontis by Victor Kraft, courtesy of Aaron Copland.

ACKNOWLEDGMENTS

Like countless others, I am deeply indebted to Mr. Aaron Copland for his extraordinary generosity. Not only did he allow me to impose on his time for interviews, but he read and corrected the final manuscript as well. I am also grateful to Mr. Leonard Bernstein for granting a most enlightening interview and sharing personal episodes of his long friendship with Aaron Copland; to Mr. Copland's music publishers, Boosey and Hawkes, Inc., as well as Mrs. Sylvia Goldstein, one of their Directors and head of their Copyright and Royalty Department; and to David Diamond of Rochester, composer.

I wish to thank the following for permission to quote material from the works indicated below: Doubleday & Co., Inc., *A Smattering of Ignorance* by Oscar Levant, 1940; E. P. Dutton & Co., Inc., *Aaron Copland: His Work and Contribution to American Music* by Julia Smith, 1955; Alfred A. Knopf, Incorporated, *The Fervent Years* by Harold Clurman, 1945; Little, Brown & Company, *Dance to the Piper* by Agnes de Mille, 1952; *The New York Times,* for short selections from musical reviews and feature articles in various issues; Oxford University Press, *Aaron Copland* by Arthur Berger, 1953.

Contents

1. People Are Nice

"May we see him, Papa? Please, Papa, may we see the new baby?"

Harris Copland nodded and herded his four other children toward the bedroom.

"Sh-h-h," he cautioned them, as he turned the knob. "Mama and the baby are both resting."

Ralph and Leon, Laurine and Josephine, tiptoed in and stood in a circle around the crib. The boys were thirteen and eleven, Laurine was nine, and Josephine, the youngest until now, was over seven. No wonder they were excited. There hadn't been a new baby in the house in so many years.

They looked down at the infant nestled in among the blankets and wrappings. Then their faces fell. He was tiny, wrinkled, reddish in color, and he was bald. Disappointed, they filed out of the room.

"Never mind," said their father with a smile. "He will grow quickly, and he will have hair. I promise you."

"What's his name?"

"His name is Aaron, for your grandfather Mittenthal."

"What will he be, Papa?"

"Who knows? First he will be a little boy, then a big boy, then a man. Now I must go down to the store. Don't bang the piano for a while."

"Not even when Uncle Alfred comes over?"

"Uncle Alfred will understand."

They watched him go down the stairs from their apartment to the family store beneath. They tiptoed through the living room to the kitchen where their housekeeper was getting dinner. How long would they have to keep quiet, they asked her. Not long, she told them. It made Laurine want to practice on the piano more than ever—because she couldn't.

Ralph just sighed and left his violin in its case.

Leon didn't mind. He was like his father, more interested in business than music.

In another few days they could make noise again. Mother was up and around and Uncle Alfred Copland visited them in the evening with his violin. They all gathered around Laurine at the piano to play and sing. They weren't really musicians. They were just a big happy family that liked to have fun together. Sometimes neighbors joined them in their fun.

Aaron Copland had been born on November 14, 1900, and he grew fast. He lost the reddish look and smiled up at his family. Soon Laurine could tell her school friends, "My new little brother is adorable."

Before they knew it he was running around—learning to talk—finding his way downstairs and into the street. He was bright and curious, and Washington Avenue in Brooklyn, New York, was an adventure. It was wide and busy. Horses trotted by pulling wagons. People crowded the sidewalk and rushed along, shopping, hurrying to work, making deliveries.

Nobody was rich on Washington Avenue, and nobody was terribly poor either. It was a street where people of many nationalities lived and got along together. Most of them came regularly into his father's store at Number 626.

Sometimes his mother took him really exploring

when she went shopping for special foods for their Jewish holidays. Clinging to her hand, he scrambled aboard a trolley car that rumbled over Brooklyn Bridge—over the wide, deep East River—to Manhattan. They were bound for the section of New York called the Lower East Side where thousands of Jewish people lived. That was where the best Jewish stores were—bakeries, butcher shops, delicatessens. But it was so crowded! People here were poor. They lived in tenements that were too small for their big families. The streets were narrow and lined with pushcarts. Some merchants didn't keep store in a building like his father. All they had were pushcarts full of merchandise standing near the curb. They shouted their wares to the shoppers. The Lower East Side seemed like a foreign world to Aaron.

The older he grew the more exploring he could do on his own. Up and down Washington Avenue he went. He found plenty of playmates to rove with him, or to play handball. He made friends with Jewish boys, Italian boys, Irish boys, Negro boys.

"We go to mass on Sunday," said a young Italian boy.

"We go to synagogue on Saturday," said Aaron. "My father is president of Beth Israel Anshei Emes."

"When I am older I shall be confirmed," said the first lad.

"And I shall have a *bar mitzvah*," Aaron replied happily.

He was usually cheerful and amiable. He had a smile that was bigger than his face, and when he smiled everybody around him did too.

But he wasn't very husky in his earliest years. If the games in the street became too rough, he perched on the front steps and watched his big brothers tumble and wrestle. If there was no game to watch, he sat on the steps and read a book.

He was quite bookish.

"Can I go to school? Can I? Can I?" he had begged when he was still too young. Each morning when his brothers and sisters piled out of the house, he watched them with big eyes. At last he was six and old enough, and his mother took him to Public School 111 on Vanderbilt Avenue. By the time he was eleven and had reached fifth grade, he went across the street to Public School 9. He could scarcely tell the difference. All schools seemed to be red brick, at least they were in Brooklyn.

Aaron liked school. He learned quickly to read and write and usually brought home good grades. But there didn't seem to be any special subject that he was keen about. What would Aaron be, his family wondered. Ralph was going to study law. Leon wanted to be a businessman.

"He'll discover something," said his father. "Let him alone."

Actually, Mr. Copland had all the expenses he could stand educating his older children. He'd worry about Aaron when the time came. Aaron was turning out to be bright enough, and he was bound to show talent somehow.

Aaron *had* shown a flair for writing when he was only in the second or third grade. He was home from school with a fever, in bed propped up on pillows. Dorothy Levy, who was Ralph's girl, had come to see him. She had talked with him and cheered him up and had even brought him some cherries. He had felt so grateful that he had written a poem for her.

"Maybe Aaron is going to be a writer," his family had said.

But that didn't seem to be it after all, and by the time he was eleven or so, Aaron wondered about his future too. Was the answer in Ralph's law books? No. In Leon's accounting books? No. In Papa's store? Well, Papa had begun to let him help in the store.

The store seemed as big as the world to Aaron. Mr. Copland had a dozen employees working for him— clerks to wait on customers, boys to unload deliveries, the cashier. There were counters and counters, full of stockings and aprons, mittens, caps, towels, tablecloths, knitting yarns, needles and thread. Papa seemed to know just what customers would ask for.

Papa liked the people who came into the store, which was just about everybody, and so did Aaron. "People are nice," they agreed.

But when stormy winter days kept people away, Aaron did have more of a chance to talk with his father.

"Tell me about Russia, Papa," he would ask.

"I came to this country when I was seventeen," his father related over and over. "My father was born in a part of Russia called Lithuania. So was your mother, but your mother and I didn't meet until we were living in America. I left Russia on my own when I was about fifteen, but I only got as far as Great Britain. I worked in Glasgow, Scotland, at every kind of job until I had earned enough for my passage. When I reached the United States I went into partnership with my cousin, and we had a dry goods store in Brooklyn."

"But Mother lived out West?"

"Yes, her family had a store in Peoria, Illinois. Then they moved to Dallas, Texas. If they hadn't decided to move again—to New York City—I never would have met her."

"It's a good thing you went to that party, Papa."

"It certainly is. What a big party! Friends and relatives, and there I heard your mother singing. Such a lovely voice! Then, when she and I were married, I went into business for myself—here."

Aaron liked to talk things over with his father, and he liked to help in the store. As he grew older Mr. Copland gave him more important tasks. Sometimes he even let Aaron help out as cashier, when the cashier went to lunch. And he always paid him for the work he did. It made Aaron feel important—and mature—and trusted.

Aaron loved his whole family, especially when they all sat around the dinner table, laughing and talking. But his favorite times were when they gathered around the piano with their friends to sing. His mother still had a singing voice, and so did his sister Laurine.

Laurine was really serious about music. She had finished high school and was studying in New York City at the Metropolitan Opera School. Aaron had no idea what that meant. The books she brought home were very different from Ralph's law books. Curious, Aaron looked through them each time.

"What is this one, Laurine?"

"That is a libretto, Aaron, the words of an opera. An opera is a play in which people sing all their lines instead of speaking them."

"But I can't read it."

"That one is in Italian. Operas are written in many languages."

Laurine often went to concerts when she was in New York. Aaron wondered what they were. She explained as well as she could, and she always remembered to bring home her program.

Aaron had never been to a concert. He had never watched a real artist play a piano or violin. Oh, there was singing at synagogue and at P.S. 9 in assembly. But it wasn't very inspiring. Laurine's eyes sparkled when she came home from a real concert.

He felt curious about music, and he often slipped into the room to watch Laurine practice. How her fingers flew over the piano! When she struck two or three keys at a time, the tones were pleasing. They seemed to melt together.

Laurine watched him out of the corner of her eye. One day she said, "Come on, Aaron; sit down and I will show you how to play the piano."

Eleven-year-old Aaron slid beside her on the bench. She spread her first lesson book in front of him.

He started to read music.

There was a staff of five lines across the page. Each note was on a line or in a space between two lines. The bottom line was E, the bottom space was F, the second line up was G, the next space was A, the next line B, the next space C, the next line D, the next space E, and the top line F.

On the piano the black keys were in groups of two

or three. The white key below the first of the two black keys was C, the next white key D, the next E, then F, then G, then A, then B, then C again.

When a note appeared on the page, in the space for C, that meant to touch C on the piano.

Music was a language, a whole new language.

Laurine showed him how to count time. The staff was divided into measures, with a certain number of counts to each measure. A waltz had three counts or beats to a measure; a march moved in two.

Laurine showed him that certain fingers belonged on certain keys of the piano. Swiftly, swiftly, it began to come to him—in lesson after lesson—and soon he could play a scale, a chord, a tune.

Discovery for Aaron Copland had begun.

2. A Born Musician

There was no end to discovery in music, and he tried to learn from everyone. Laurine gave him all the time she could spare. His mother played some piano and sang. Uncle Alfred knew a lot about the violin; so did Ralph.

Aaron worked so hard and learned so fast that at last Laurine said, "I can't teach you any more."

All that she had needed four years to learn, her brother had gobbled up in six months.

It was just as well that the lessons stopped, because

Aaron was original as well as brilliant. He had begun to disagree with Laurine. Why must it be *that* way? Why did he have to obey rules? Why couldn't he play the piece to suit himself?

"Because, Aaron, the composer wrote it *this* way."

He went on practicing the piano by himself. It became more important than ever to earn money in his father's store so that he could buy sheet music to play. He practiced and he worked for a year and a half. He knew he was pretty good, but he felt he wasn't getting anywhere fast enough. He seemed to be just floundering around, and he was impatient to learn.

"I want to study with a real teacher," he told his parents.

His father and mother both shook their heads. Music lessons were expensive. They had spent about all they could on Laurine and Ralph. Putting Ralph through law school had been very costly.

But Aaron was on fire. He knew what he wanted. He pestered his father in the store, or followed his mother around the apartment, pestering her.

Finally she said, "Oh, all right. If you will find yourself a piano teacher, we will pay for lessons."

Aaron was off like a shot, to talk to his friends and relatives. Who taught piano in Brooklyn? He wanted someone who was good, very good! At last, with the help of his big family, he learned that Leopold Wolfsohn—a teacher with a fine reputation—came to a Brooklyn studio one day a week at 345 Clinton Avenue. That was five blocks down Washington Avenue and then two over.

Eagerly Aaron strode through the streets to the address. Clinton Avenue—he discovered—was wide and lovely, with mansions on each side and no stores. At one of those big old houses, Aaron Copland knocked on the door.

Then he went limp.

"Suppose he won't have me? Suppose he says I have no talent?"

The man who appeared at the door looked just like an artist. He wore a velvet smoking jacket and a shirt with an open collar. He had gray, wavy hair and a high forehead, and Aaron could tell right way that his character was firm.

Mr. Wolfsohn stood looking at the skinny boy with his brown hair brushed back, intense blue eyes, a large nose, and a wide mouth.

"Come in," he said, and when they were inside, "Play something for me."

Aaron must have seemed talented, because Mr. Wolfsohn agreed to give him piano lessons.

"You are rather old to start out working toward a concert career," Wolfsohn warned him.

"I'll make it up! I'll make it up!"

Mr. Wolfsohn was a fine teacher. Aaron was a hard-working student. They got on well together. Mr. Wolfsohn guided Aaron as his young student drove ahead into a whole new world. To Aaron music was the most wonderful of arts. Music could express every thought and feeling known to man. It had no limits. Every new detail that he learned was exciting. Why, just the way he held his fingers and wrists made such a difference!

Music was both a science and an art. Rhythms and tones could be put together in designs to create all sorts of effects. The more you knew, the more designs you could invent.

Mr. Wolfsohn gave him Chopin waltzes to learn. Until then a waltz had been a very simple kind of dance that he and his family hummed around the piano or danced to. Just an easy, *one*-two-three, *one*-two-three, over and over. On the piano the left hand kept time with a low note and two thumps, a low note and two thumps, while the right hand diddled out the melody.

But Chopin's waltzes were complicated, and the left hand had to do just as much work as the right. Chopin decorated the melody with trills and runs and grace notes, from one end of the piano to the other. His waltzes were charming and refined. They were sometimes sad, sometimes gay, always romantic.

Then Aaron Copland moved on to learn pieces

written by Mozart and Beethoven. They were different from each other, but in both he found new kinds of beauty.

Mozart's music was delicate and controlled. It was put together like the works of a fine watch. Sometimes when Aaron was struggling to learn a Mozart sonata, he felt like cheering. Just looking at the page was a joy.

The sonata, he learned, was completely different from the waltz. Its rhythms were different, and it was longer. A sonata usually had three parts. In the first part the composer set down his ideas, or melodies, and that part was usually fast and snappy. The next was often slow, and in it the composer developed his more serious ideas, added variations and decorations. Part three was fast again, often exciting. It was really the wrap-up.

Aaron knew he was living when he had learned to play some of Mozart's piano pieces—until he came to Beethoven. Beethoven was just as great as Mozart, but much more dramatic. His music was controlled— when he wanted it to be. But he could also let himself go—really *go!* He could make the piano speak in a whisper or thunder like drums.

When Aaron Copland was learning to play a work by Mozart or Beethoven, measure by measure, he forgot everything else. What craftsmen these composers were. How much they had to know to write a sonata.

Fancy knowing how to write original music. Just fancy it!

Aaron Copland could dream. He could take long rides on pink clouds. But he was a practical person too. All the while he was studying with Mr. Wolfsohn, he went to P.S. 9 during the day and often helped in the store after school. Warm weather found him on the front steps reading or playing handball in the street. Religious holidays found him at the synagogue with his family.

His *bar mitzvah*, when he was thirteen, was to be an important religious day in his life. All the members of his family, his relations and his friends, would celebrate his coming of age. From then on he would be a responsible adult in everyone's eyes. After a solemn ceremony at the synagogue, his parents would give him a party, the guests bringing him presents. He would rise and address everyone, giving a speech that he had learned by heart.

As he and his parents made up the list of those to invite, it grew longer and longer.

"How many relatives do I have?" asked Aaron.

"Too many to count," said Mr. Copland.

And he wanted his neighborhood friends too.

"Which ones do you want?" his mother asked.

"I like them *all*," he told her.

"I like them all too," said his father, "and I know how we will solve this."

He turned the store into a banquet hall. The employees moved the counters and dry goods back and filled the entire store with long tables.

It all seemed fine until the day arrived. Then, while guests came filing in—happy, congratulating him—Aaron wondered about the speech he would have to make. Suppose he forgot! Suppose they couldn't hear him. The store had never seemed so big. But it all went off well. Aaron spoke and then sat down to happy applause and cheers.

And so back to his schoolwork and his music. By the time Aaron was fourteen all of his brothers and sisters were married with homes of their own. He had the piano all to himself.

He graduated from P.S. 9 in June, 1914, and entered Boys' High School on Marcy Avenue that same fall. But by then music had become so important to him that he was neglecting his lessons. Not only did he study less, but high school subjects were more difficult. Some of the subjects—Latin and mathematics, for instance—didn't interest him much. But he was glad for his French course. He knew French was important in music.

There was a musical test looming ahead of him that

was a much bigger challenge than speaking at his *bar mitzvah*. Mr. Wolfsohn gave a recital every year at which his students had to perform. Naturally, the parents who were paying for the lessons wanted to hear how their children were getting along. The recital was the time for that.

Aaron was at work on "Polonaise" by Paderewski. A polonaise is a dance that used to be performed in royal courts. It is full of rhythm, and this one had tricky passages where Aaron could show off his skill.

Aaron practiced. His parents planned. He must have a new suit and look his best. After all, the recital was to be in the Wanamaker Auditorium, across the river in Manhattan. Even his parents had begun to suspect that Aaron was finding his career.

The practicing, the plans, the excitement, were all pure joy—until the day of the recital—until those last few moments before he had to go out on the stage. Standing in the wings, awaiting his turn to go on, Aaron suddenly realized that Mr. Wolfsohn was behind him. Mr. Wolfsohn understood stage fright. All the progress a student had made could vanish when he stepped out in front of that sea of staring faces. The teacher began to box his student's ears to shake him out of it, telling him: "Don't be nervous!" It made Aaron just a little angry, and that was the cure.

"I am not nervous," Aaron retorted. "Let me alone!"

The applause for the last number died away. He was on—walking across that huge stage—making a brief bow before sitting down at the piano. What he saw out there was not a sea of staring faces, but people. Instead of scaring him, they made him want to love them. As he poised his hands above the keyboard, he began to fill with a warm, friendly feeling. He and they were going to enjoy music together. He played—for them—and the brilliant Polish dance went well. He did it better than he had ever done it before.

"Aaron is a born musician," Mr. Wolfsohn decided. He knew that he had to convince Aaron's family that they must do all they could to help Aaron after that.

3. I Want to Be a Composer

Aaron intended to help himself. He would work and save his money. Perhaps when he played well enough he could play the piano somewhere for pay. Of one thing he was certain: music was going to be his life, somehow. He was going to learn all he could about music—from every angle.

Up came an angle.

Ignace Jan Paderewski, the Polish composer who had written "Polonaise" was coming to Brooklyn to give a concert. He was on one of his American tours.

Aaron had never been to a concert. He realized that watching and listening to great artists perform was another way to learn about music. Climbing aboard a trolley car, he rattled downtown to the Brooklyn Academy of Music to buy a ticket.

On the night of the concert, he found the street in front of the Academy teeming with excited crowds. They had all come to hear the great pianist-composer. Aaron Copland crowded into the lobby, handed his ticket to the ticket-taker, and moved into the huge hall. His mouth was so dry he could hardly swallow.

The lights dimmed, and the audience hushed until it was silent. A gentle, slender little man walked out upon the stage. Applause thundered. Paderewski was humble. He nodded and took his place at the piano. For this program the hall was dark except for a single floor lamp upon the stage. Eerie and mysterious! Until Paderewski began to play. A gentle, slender little man? He was a lion at the piano. The most exciting piece that he played was Chopin's "Revolutionary Étude," but the whole program was a tremendous experience that swept over Aaron like a tidal wave.

When it was over, fifteen-year-old Aaron struggled through the milling audience to the door. He rushed out into the cool night air. His head burned; his heart pounded. Paderewski played music; he wrote music. Composer-pianist! Pianist-composer! Both! This was

what he had been thinking about for some time without realizing it. Now he knew what he wanted to be—
a composer.

When he told his parents, they shook their heads and looked at one another. Aaron had chosen a long, hard road to travel. Perhaps the idea would wear off.

Mr. Wolfsohn didn't have much to say about it either. But he was sympathetic. He went on teaching and guiding Aaron.

Naturally, Aaron talked to his friends about it. To one especially—Aaron Schaffer.

The two Aarons had met one summer at a lake in the Catskill Mountains in New York State. The Copland family went somewhere every year on vacation, and they liked the Catskills.

Schaffer, a passionate music-lover, enjoyed hearing Aaron practice on the hotel piano. Even though he was seven years older, he found Aaron Copland so gifted and remarkable that he had to know him better—that is, when he could get him away from the piano.

They became friends right away. Aaron Copland shared all his musical thoughts with his new friend. Young Schaffer gave him just the kind of sympathy and understanding he needed. Copland was already trying to write original music, but he couldn't get very far with it. He produced only bits and pieces.

"You need more technical training," said his new friend.

At the end of the summer they agreed to keep in touch. Schaffer had to return to Baltimore, where he continued his studies at Johns Hopkins University.

Another friend was John Kober, who also went to Boys' High School. He studied music too. John and Aaron roamed around Brooklyn together—talking about everything under the sun—mostly music. They roamed down Montague Street one day and stopped in front of an old red-stone building—the Brooklyn Public Library.

"Do you suppose they have any books on music?"

"Let's find out."

In they went.

The music was upstairs, said the librarian.

Up they went, two wooden steps at a time. They discovered a whole collection that most people never bothered with: books about the history of music, biographies of great composers, opera scores.

"May we borrow these?"

"Yes, these books circulate."

Sheet music, piano solos, and piano duets that he and John Kober could play together also circulated.

After that the library became one of Aaron Copland's friends.

Aaron had friends who didn't realize they were his friends. Walter Damrosch, the conductor, was one. Dr. Damrosch led the New York Symphony Orchestra; he and his orchestra gave a concert every month at the Brooklyn Academy of Music. Aaron Copland went.

Young Copland never forgot the first time he actually *saw* and *heard* a symphony orchestra. Not just one artist, but a whole orchestra gradually came out upon the stage and took their places. Aaron observed all the different instruments and how they were arranged—in families. On the left all the first and second violins sat bunched together. In back of them were the kettle-drums. In the center of the stage sat the men who played the wind instruments: flutes, oboes, clarinets, and bassoons; the trumpets, trombones, brass horns, and tubas. To the right were the big stringed instruments: cellos, bull fiddles, and harps. When they played it was "musical glory," he said later. One man, the conductor, controlled all of them with a stick or baton. To do it he had the conductor's score on the stand before him.

The next time he was in the library, Aaron Copland dug out a conductor's score for a symphony and sat looking at it—mouth open. Wow! How many heads did a conductor need to follow that?

There was a staff of five lines for each instrument or

group of instruments. In the case of a drum that had only one tone, the staff became a single line.

Could he ever learn to write a score for a whole orchestra? He most certainly did not have enough technical knowledge yet. The composer had to write the music for every instrument in the orchestra. He had to think of all the instruments at once and imagine how they would sound together.

Program after program, Aaron listened and watched as Dr. Damrosch conducted pieces by such composers as Mozart, Bach, Beethoven, and Chopin. He studied the back of Damrosch's white head, the motions of his arms. Most of all, he watched the way the musicians collaborated with him. That was how to get perfect results.

And Aaron would strive for perfect results—by practicing and studying—by going to concerts, concerts, concerts.

He burst in upon his mother one day with great news.

"John McCormack is coming to the Hippodrome in New York to sing! He's the Irish tenor."

Yes, yes, she knew. Who did not know about the great McCormack?

"You are going with me, Mother. You will be my guest this time. My treat."

She could hardly say *no*.

That marvelous voice—warm, clear, rich. A singing voice was a gift straight from God, he and his mother agreed.

Listening to McCormack made Aaron think of all the singing he knew about—his mother's voice, his sister's studies at the Metropolitan Opera School, the librettos of operas that she used to bring home and explain. An opera was a play in which all the characters sang their words. He had never been to an opera, never heard human voices and orchestra together. He'd have to do that. He'd have to see an opera some day.

By the end of his sophomore year in high school "some day" seemed very far off. A war that had begun in Europe in 1914 was growing worse. It changed everybody's plans everywhere in the world—somehow. Most of the countries of Europe had joined one side or the other. The Allies were England, France, Belgium, and Russia, and they were at war against Germany and Austria.

Aaron Copland, John Kober, and the rest of the students at Boys' High sat in assembly one morning. A speaker told them about the war in Europe. The armies of Germany and Austria had driven westward through Belgium and into northern France. The people of Belgium and the occupied part of France were starving, because the invading armies had seized all their crops and farm animals. The free world, especially America, was doing all it could to produce extra food and send it to the starving adults and children in Europe. Would the young men of Boys' High volunteer to help with the harvest this summer?

Aaron thought of his hands; heavy farm work would stiffen them. He thought of going all summer without practicing on the piano. He thought of the starving people in France and Belgium, especially the children. Then he volunteered.

He was assigned to help pick the berry crop in Marlboro, New York. As it turned out picking berries wasn't very hard on the hands. And—one of the local families owned a piano.

Aaron perked up the minute he heard it. Maybe if he were very polite about it, they would let him play once in a while. He found the house and knocked. When the man opened the door, Aaron turned on the charm full blast—including the smile that was as contagious as measles.

"Come in, young man," he was told.

A few words and he had permission to practice every day. In a confidential letter to John Kober he said the piano was a "tin pan," but that didn't matter. It had a keyboard on which he could exercise his fingers.

In the spring of 1917—Aaron's junior year—the United States became involved and declared war on Germany. American troops began to go abroad to fight. That meant a real shortage of manpower on the farms, and so high school boys volunteered once more—including Aaron.

"Am back here again . . . and living in a barn," he wrote John Kober. "After picking berries all day we cook our meal and go for a swim."

When he returned to Brooklyn in the fall, Mr. Wolfsohn was deeply pleased that he had kept up with his practicing. Aaron had also been struggling to write his own original music, but he wasn't getting on any better than when he had talked with Aaron Schaffer about it. He realized more than ever that he needed technical training.

Aaron had already tried to take a correspondence course in the subject. But he just couldn't get on fast enough by mail. He wanted personal and individual instruction.

"I want to study harmony," he told Mr. Wolfsohn.

Mr. Wolfsohn nodded. Harmony was essential. It meant far more than striking three, four, or five keys on the piano and having them melt into a pleasing tone. It was a progression of chords. There was a whole harmonic make-up of a piece of music that a composer must understand.

"I don't know where to find such a teacher," Aaron said.

"I will help you," Mr. Wolfsohn replied. "I shall give you a letter to Mr. Rubin Goldmark in New York City. He is one of the best."

This would not mean a change of teachers, because Mr. Goldmark was a specialist in harmony. If Aaron studied with Mr. Goldmark, he would continue his regular lessons with Mr. Wolfsohn at the same time.

4. New Music

When Aaron Copland started out for Manhattan to see Mr. Goldmark, he was beginning a new part of his life. Down in the subway he was pushed and jostled and mashed, but he was busy wondering just what this teacher would be like. At Times Square he struggled out of the express train and crossed the platform to a local train. Mr. Goldmark's studio was on West 87th Street.

Feeling a little queasy, he rang the doorbell. Mr.

Goldmark was well known. He didn't take anybody or everybody for a pupil. The door flew open, and a maid told him to wait. The waiting room was large, with a great many chairs.

In came an important-looking man.

"Well, young man, what's the matter with you?" he growled. At least it sounded like a growl.

"Nothing, sir. I want to study harmony."

"You want to see my brother. Better ring the other bell."

He was Dr. Carl Goldmark, not Mr. Rubin Goldmark.

Aaron did as he was told, and the next door that opened to him was the right one.

Rubin Goldmark was a heavy-set man, with a round face, a big mustache, and wide, deep eyes. He was bald on top and had a big cigar in his mouth.

The first question *he* asked was, "What do you want to become a composer for?"

Aaron didn't have much of an answer ready. He wanted to be a composer because he knew he had to be. Music was the thing for him.

Mr. Goldmark invited him to sit down. They chatted and laughed and joked until the young student was at ease.

"Now we will go to the piano."

Suddenly Rubin Goldmark was all business, deadly

serious. Aaron Copland realized quickly that he would be a strict teacher. With him you were either excellent or you were nothing. Well, that was what he wanted.

To work with Mr. Goldmark was to learn the science of putting notes of music together. He must learn all the grammar of music. Composing original music was a fine and complicated craft.

He already knew that the three elements of music are rhythm, melody, and harmony.

Rhythm was the oldest. It was the beat. It was keeping time. It went back to the first jungle drums. After a staff of five lines is divided into equal sections or measures, the next step is to decide how many beats to a measure: two, three, four, five. A waltz has three beats to a measure; a march has two. The first beat is usually stressed. BOOM-da-da, or BOOM-da. So far as Aaron could see there was no limit to the ways in which a composer could vary rhythm. He could make a measure have six, eight, nine, twelve beats if he liked. He could do anything with rhythm, if he had imagination enough.

And he had no trouble understanding melody. That was the tune or theme, the idea on which the whole composition was based. Chopin's waltzes were full of melodies. Chopin had shown him how many ways a composer can take a melody or theme and vary it, decorate it, change it around, or combine it with other melodies. Mozart had shown him how delicately it can be done.

When he came to harmony he had to slow down and admit that Mr. Wolfsohn was right. He didn't know very much about it. But with Mr. Goldmark to guide him, he learned. Harmony meant discovering all the possible ways that chords are formed, and how they can be made to build the skeletal frame of a piece of music.

Mr. Goldmark insisted that the notes in harmony must be spaced in certain ways to sound right. The notes C, E, and G, for instance, made a good combination. Aaron felt rebellious about this. Who made these rules? What would happen to him if he struck two keys right next to each other on the piano? But he didn't know enough yet to argue about it.

Harmony meant much more. He learned to play one melody with the right hand, another melody with the left. The two harmonized with each other. There was no limit—absolutely no limit—to the ways that two or more melodies could be woven together to make beautiful sounds.

Mozart did this the most beautifully of any composer that Aaron had studied so far. He and Mr. Goldmark could agree on that.

"Study the sonatas of Mozart, Haydn, and Beethoven," Mr. Goldmark insisted. "The sonata is the finest design there is for a piece of music."

Once more Aaron felt rebellious. Oh, he loved Haydn, Mozart, and Beethoven, and he loved playing sonatas. But there were many other forms that music could take. There were waltzes, lullabies, marches, operas, symphonies, and probably others that he hadn't heard of yet.

He knew Mr. Goldmark was a fine teacher, and Aaron was a kindly, warmhearted person who seldom quarreled with anyone. He just decided to find out about every kind of musical form in every way possible. New York City was full of opportunities, and he was there every Saturday morning for his music lesson. He read the music magazines and watched for advertisements of concerts. The only real problem was that he couldn't go to them all.

Aaron had promised himself that "some day" he would see an opera. So one of the first things he did when he started to take lessons in Manhattan was to subscribe to a seat at the Metropolitan Opera every other Wednesday evening. When he learned that his first opera would be something called *Boris Godunov,* he rushed to the library to read about it in advance: the libretto and the music score too. They were *out!* Obviously, other ticket-holders had had the same idea.

Aaron Copland had no idea what to expect when he entered the opera house. All he knew was that Boris Godunov was the name of the hero in the opera by a Russian composer named Mussorgsky. What he saw and heard and felt was a miracle.

The first scene was in front of a cathedral in Moscow. Crowds were gathered to witness the coronation of Boris as Tsar of Russia. Aaron's parents had come from Russia! He was looking at one of the squares of the Kremlin with onion-shaped tops on the towers. The costumes were of olden times, and Boris wore a long golden gown studded with precious stones.

Aaron watched wide-eyed and listened. The entire company, singing the coronation hymn, held him spell-bound. At one point the giant bells of the cathedral pealed and tolled as the chorus sang. How many bells were there? Six? A dozen? He couldn't tell. He was hearing all sorts of musical instruments that he hadn't thought about before—cymbals, chimes, bells.

The opera was long, but Aaron Copland heard every note and voice. Boris had a deep bass voice; Gregory, the villain, was a tenor. Boris's two children sang soprano. On the opera went, through the revolt of the peasants, the death of Boris, and the bells again.

Opera! Music drama! Orchestra and people playing, singing, and acting all at the same time.

Aaron Copland left the opera house exhausted and

happy. He'd never miss a night at the opera. Never! How he wished he could come to New York more often. But he still had his senior year at Boys' High to finish.

That same winter another important experience happened to him—the music of Claude Debussy. The Philadelphia Orchestra was giving a concert at Carnegie Hall, and Aaron went.

As usual he sat down and looked over his program. He rather wondered about the pieces by someone named Debussy. Well, he'd find out.

The orchestra played two of Debussy's nocturnes: "Nuages" (Clouds) and "Fêtes" (Festivals). Suddenly Aaron Copland was alive, excited. What was he hearing? Were his ears deceiving him? Debussy's music broke the conventional rules of harmony, yet it was beautiful. Its rhythms were fascinating, and its melodies were rich and fluent. Debussy's music flowed smoothly, like smoke curling up into the air when there is no wind. "Clouds" was a slow piece, as slow as clouds moving across a sky. "Festivals" was swift, gay, and it made him think of dancers in bright-colored skirts— whirling around, promenading, whirling again.

Aaron had to know more about Debussy.

"Try the music library on East Fifty-eighth Street," someone told him, and he found the entire upper floor of the library devoted to music.

Debussy, he learned, was French, and he belonged to the present, not the olden past. Until this spring of 1918 he had lived in Paris. Debussy had learned all he could from the masters—Bach, Haydn, Mozart, Beethoven—and then had gone on to create his own original kind of music. He strove to create impressions or pictures: a faun playing his pipes, dancing fairies, a garden in the rain. Other young composers were following him, revolting against old-fashioned music.

Knowing about one modern composer sent Aaron searching for others, and he found them: Scriabin, Stravinsky, Bartók, Ravel. All strange names that he had not known about before.

Their music was full of surprises, and sometimes it was shocking. But the composers all had one thing in common: they were original. They had the courage to be different, to be themselves. If a composer of the "new music" wanted to strike two keys on the piano right next to each other to get the effect he wanted, he did it. Debussy threw away the book of rules and composed harmonies that he *liked*.

Because of Debussy and others France was becoming the leading influence in music.

"I want to go to Paris to study," Aaron Copland decided. "I want to learn to write my own different and original music."

He saved his money all the harder, because a trip that far would cost a great deal. His French classes in high school seemed more important now.

He always gabbed at home about his plans, and when he announced that he wanted to go to Paris, his father just said, "You will have to wait for the war to end."

Mr. Goldmark had some advice to give too. Aaron still had a great deal to learn about the rules of composition before he could think of breaking them.

At last, in June, 1918, Aaron Copland graduated. He had grown tall during his four years in high school and was no longer a skinny boy. He felt and thought like an adult too. Now was the logical time to talk over his situation with his family.

"I want to go on with music," he told them, and they weren't a bit surprised.

"What about college?" his parents wanted to know. "We would like you to have a college education."

But Aaron wanted to devote all of his time to music. His first year of studying in New York had given him a tantalizing taste of all that was going on. He had read in the musical magazines about the New York Philharmonic Orchestra, about the Boston Symphony Orchestra. He had actually seen the Philadelphia Orchestra the night he had first heard Debussy's music. And there were great singers like Enrico Caruso, Amelita

Galli-Curci, and Mary Garden—all performing in New York. A young Russian composer named Prokofiev was going to tour the United States with the Russian Symphony Society.

"If I were away at college I'd miss all these programs!" Aaron explained to his family.

He'd keep up with his reading and improve his education, he promised them. And he'd earn money at part-time jobs. They wouldn't have to bear the whole burden.

His parents gave their consent. The whole family was with him, in fact—all his married brothers and sisters, not to mention his aunts and uncles. They would help him either to become a composer or get it out of his system.

Young Copland continued to live at home and take the subway to Manhattan for his music lessons, concerts, and operas. He read new books and the important magazines on literature and world affairs—and especially on music.

He knew in his heart that he was going to do something important some day. He must prepare himself carefully.

5. *I Am Coming!*

He must earn money, too, if he was ever going to pay
for that trip to Paris. Practical and with a good head
for business, Aaron soon had a job with Bache & Co.
as a Wall Street runner for the summer months. Ami-
ably he sat on a bench with the other runners, waiting
for an assignment. Take these stocks to this address.
Carry this bundle of papers to that place or other. His
employer kept him on the hop—really running.

But his lunch hour was his own. Then he could roam

the narrow, crowded streets of downtown Manhattan. It didn't take him long to find secondhand bookstores. Rummaging and rooting through the bins of old books, he came up with a treasure: a book written in French, his first.

By the time his summer job ended, the winter music season began. And that same November of 1918 the war ended. France would soon be at peace. He could really hope to see Paris.

"You aren't ready yet," Mr. Goldmark told him, and Aaron knew that his teacher was right. He must do a lot more work on the fine points of harmony, the larger forms of composition, not to mention orchestration.

And he must practice. Not a day went by without a few hours at the piano.

And he must earn money.

He studied the want-ad columns in the Brooklyn papers and discovered that someone needed a pianist. He applied and soon went on the interview. The job would be playing with a small orchestra at the Finnish Socialist Hall in Brooklyn. The room where the group met was big with very little furniture, almost like a gymnasium, because the members of the club liked to dance.

They were all ages, but Aaron enjoyed most talking with the young intellectuals, especially Arne Vainio, who had hired him. Vainio played both clarinet and cello. He was keenly interested in new music and new poetry.

"Of course, the old masters are fine and wonderful. But there must be new masters in every generation. The old masters lived in romantic times, and so they wrote romantic music and poetry. But these are different times. We need different composers and poets who understand *us*."

They gabbed and gabbed—about new music and poetry—and new political ideas too, especially socialism.

Aaron told his father about that the way he did everything else. His father was stern.

"America has the only real idea when it comes to government," he wanted Aaron to remember.

Aaron didn't really want to change the American government. He just felt excited by so much originality. The Socialist Club did two things for him. It gave him a chance to earn money as a musician, and it made him try harder to write original music. He was interested to hear about radical politics. But he wanted to *be* a radical composer.

Like Debussy. . . .

And like the new Russian composer who had just come to New York to play his radical music: Sergei Prokofiev.

Prokofiev was still in his twenties, tall and fair. At Aeolian Hall he gave a recital of his own music and of other modern composers. His music was so new and startling that one critic said you needed a new set of ears to listen to it. Critics wrote reams and reams trying to explain him. That in itself made him important. Prokofiev could make the piano express any emotion: fierce hatred, tender love, joy, despair. He could do it because he used the newest methods in composing, and he had a terrific imagination.

A revolution was happening in music, and Aaron Copland was part of it. Every time he tried to compose something of his own he grew more and more a part of it. There came a day when he completed a piece that he thought might be satisfactory. Naturally, he gave it a French title, "Le Chat et la Souris" (The Cat and the Mouse). It was a short piano solo, and he showed it to Mr. Goldmark.

But Mr. Goldmark was too conservative.

"I have no standards by which to judge such modern experiments," was all he could offer.

Well, at least he hadn't said it was bad.

"I'll take it with me to Paris some day," Copland decided.

Some day, some day!

When his friend Aaron Schaffer wrote from Baltimore and said, "I am going to study at the Sorbonne," Aaron Copland thought he would fall apart. The Sorbonne was the University of Paris.

"You must visit us in Brooklyn before you go abroad," he wrote back. "I want to hear all about your plans."

His friend accepted, and the two Aarons had some happy hours together before Schaffer sailed.

"Please play for me," said Aaron Schaffer.

The younger Aaron did, and when he had finished his friend was frankly amazed.

"You are a real virtuoso!"

Soon Schaffer wrote from Paris, "I know you would find joy in this city if you were here; the concerts are simply countless."

Everything seemed to be drawing him toward Paris and French music—even a French opera. The Chicago Opera Company came to New York. One of its programs was to be *Pelléas et Mélisande* by Debussy. Aaron got in line right away in front of the box office of the Lexington Theatre. He stood and waited until at last he reached the window and bought a ticket.

At that moment he wished just what he had wished many other times—that another music student were going with him. Oh, he would talk a blue streak to his family about it afterward. But none of them knew as much about music as he did now. In high school he had had plenty of classmates in history, Latin, and math. They could talk over their homework together. He longed for music classmates.

On Wednesday night, January 28, 1920, he climbed up to his balcony seat and looked down on the audience. People were chatting and waiting for the music to begin. In the expensive seats down in front, many wore evening clothes. Suddenly there was a flurry of excitement. A white-haired gentleman, who must have been in his late sixties, had entered one of the boxes.

"Who is that?" Aaron asked someone near him.

"That is Count Maurice Maeterlinck who wrote the play, *Pelléas et Mélisande*. He is seeing it as an opera for the first time."

Aaron cared more about the music. He had studied a lot about Debussy by then. He knew that Debussy had worked on this opera for many years, revising and changing. And he knew that Mary Garden, who was singing the role of Mélisande, had gone to Paris to rehearse with Monsieur Debussy himself.

At last the house lights were lowered and the orchestra began—slow, meaningful chords, full of foreboding and suspense. Then the voices—the baritone. Or was he a tenor? No, Aaron thought baritone. And Mary Garden's high, delicate soprano. Voices and music flowed along together, building excitement and suspense. The opera was full of melodic phrases, the kind of melody that seemed to start and never end.

Aaron's emotions were so deep and intense after the curtains closed on the last scene that he walked for blocks in the cold night air. The music, the voices, the death scene! The whole opera had a feeling of mystery about it.

After that he watched the music columns in the papers and the music magazines more closely than ever. Until one day he read an advertisement in the magazine, *Musical America,* that changed his life.

There was to be a summer school in France for American music students: the Fontainebleau School of Music for Americans. It had been started by the French government, the Ministry of Beaux Arts, the town of Fontainebleau, and a group in the United States called American Friends of Musicians in France. The director was the renowned organist, Charles-Marie Widor, and Walter Damrosch was vice president of the American group. Walter Damrosch's influence had had a lot to do with starting the project.

This pink cloud was the most solid Aaron Copland had ever been on. But how to afford it? There were scholarships, said the ad. Aaron wrote at once for the catalogue. When the postman finally delivered the envelope, Aaron sat right down and filled out the application.

Then the apartment up over the store was really in a hubbub, until the notice came that he had been granted a scholarship. After that the hubbub was worse than ever. *All* of his big family, *all* of his friends and neighbors had to know about it. He was going to France! He would spend the whole summer studying at the school in Fontainebleau. Then he would go to Paris and stay as long as his money held out.

"I am coming!" he wrote to Aaron Schaffer, who was still in Paris.

"I am truly delighted!" the other Aaron wrote back.

6. France

But the other Aaron was returning to America soon, and fortunately he was due back well before Aaron Copland's departure. There was plenty of time for a visit at the Coplands' apartment in Brooklyn.

Young Aaron couldn't stop asking the older man questions and more questions about the city and country he was about to see. "Tell me about living in Paris! Do you think my French is good enough now? Can I rent a cheap room to make my money last longer? Is Fontainebleau far from Paris? What kind of food do they eat? Is it very cold in winter?"

Aaron Schaffer knew perfectly well how thrilling Paris was going to be, and he tried to answer every question.

Yes, his friend's French seemed adequate. He could live most cheaply in the section called the Left Bank, near the Sorbonne. There were inexpensive hotels there. Once settled, he could soon find a permanent place to live. Fontainebleau was less than an hour away from Paris.

Even after Aaron Schaffer left, the happy, excited gabbing went on. So did all the preparations. And people were continually dropping in to congratulate Aaron —friends and relatives—for just about everybody had heard of his scholarship.

"I want you to meet my brother-in-law," said Elsie Clurman, a cousin. "He is going to study at the Sorbonne soon, and you and he can be friends over there."

Her brother-in-law turned out to be Harold Clurman, now the famous drama critic and Broadway director. In that spring of 1921 he was just another young hopeful who didn't know much more about Paris and France than Aaron Copland. But they could talk about plans. Aaron was sailing on June 9, 1921, and Clurman wasn't going until the fall.

"I am spending the summer in Fontainebleau, but I should be back in Paris by the time you get there," said Copland. "I'll find a small apartment that we can share.

Would you like that? It will be cheaper for both of us."

Clurman agreed.

The next few weeks were full of firsts for Aaron Copland.

First time aboard an ocean-going ship!

He was sailing on the S.S. *France* with the group of students who had been chosen for Fontainebleau. As he stood at the rail waving to people far down on the dock, he wondered why they were crying. This was a happy time! At last the ship pulled away from the dock and made her way down through New York harbor, past the Statue of Liberty, and out onto the Atlantic Ocean—out of sight of land.

He strolled along the deck with his new friends, feeling the ship move beneath his feet, adjusting his steps to its motion. They were all traveling third class, so their quarters were way below the water line, six bunks to a cabin.

"Let's explore!" And they did.

"There's a room with a piano in it."

"I think that's called a salon."

They took their meals in a dining salon, and other passengers took a lot of interest in them. Aaron Copland was now an attractive adult, going on twenty-one. He had begun to wear glasses and they made him look older. With his usual flair for getting on easily with people, he soon became acquainted with several prominent persons abroad. One of them was the famous French painter, Marcel Duchamp. Duchamp was a man in his thirties, and the way he puffed his cigar and talked with his eyes partly closed made him seem very worldly to Aaron. Duchamp loved to discuss "new art." In fact, he had been one of the leaders in the new art movement for at least ten years. He broke old-fashioned rules and painted pictures so original they shocked people. That was to make them think. He was striving to free art from the past, to give it more real value for the present day.

Duchamp took a real interest in Aaron Copland and gave him a lot of advice about living in Paris, especially on the Left Bank, where everything was cheaper.

The high point of the voyage for Aaron Copland was being asked to participate in a concert. Passengers in the first-class section had planned a program, and they wanted Mr. Copland to play a piano solo. The sea was a little choppy that evening, and Aaron felt a bit seasick, but he managed to get off Beethoven's sonata Opus 90 fairly well. At least, the audience seemed to like it.

Then. . . .

First sight of France!

The northern coast of France that bordered on the English Channel looked flat, curving, misty brownish, as the ship approached the harbor of Le Havre. In the

far distance Aaron could see some low bluish mountains. But he had time for only quick glances. There
was much bustling and hurrying as the ship moved
inside the sea walls that formed the breakwater. As
soon as the S.S. *France* was made fast to the pier, Aaron
Copland hurried with the rest of the passengers down
the gangplank and aboard a boat-train that would take
them up to Paris.

The French countryside rolled gently past the train
window. There was an industrial town with tall chim-
neys sending up black smoke. He saw a stone cottage
with a thatched roof—a farmer wearing baggy trousers.
France seemed meadowy—and misty. There was a
town of little stone houses and a church spire rising in
the midst of them—then more hills, a sprinkling of trees,
a stretch of woods, and . . . a city . . . the city . . .
Debussy's city.

First time in Paris!

The railroad station was bustling and crowded like
one in America. He picked up his luggage and hurried
down a long flight of stairs to a street just as bustling
and just as crowded. He was utterly alone—didn't know
a soul in Paris. Hailing a taxi, he told the driver in
French to take him to the Hotel Savoy in the rue de
Vaugirard. And his French worked!

As the little taxi rattled along he stretched his neck
this way and that. There was the Eiffel Tower rising

in the distance—and the River Seine curving through the heart of the city. The taxi crossed one of the many bridges to the south side of Paris, the Left Bank, where so many artists lived.

His hotel was in a section called Montparnasse where the streets ran at odd angles to each other and the buildings were so old they sometimes leaned a little. Many were decorated with carved stone designs; some had black iron balconies in front of the upper windows.

As soon as he had put down his bags, Aaron Copland hurried downstairs and back into the streets—to see more of Montparnasse, more of the Left Bank section of Paris. He was *here!* And he had a whole week to roam about and explore before going on to Fontainebleau. He could tell at once that he and Harold Clurman could easily find a cheap apartment in this part of town.

The Sorbonne, he discovered, was just a few blocks away. The Sorbonne with its many buildings—some rather new, some going way back into history—was really the University of Paris, nearly seven hundred years old. He soon found the rue Mouffetard, where street vendors had their wares for sale in carts along the edge of the curb. It reminded him of the Lower East Side in New York. He and Clurman could come here to shop for food and do their own cooking. That would save a lot of money. How the vendors shouted, trying to compete with each other. "Come buy my fine cheese!" "Fresh fish, fresh fish!" Some of the calls were musical.

Wandering back to the Seine River he discovered counters full of secondhand books all along the Left Bank. And out in the middle of the river, on an island, stood the mighty Cathedral of Notre Dame.

Oh, he was looking forward to coming back to Paris in the fall. Then he'd have plenty of time to browse through the secondhand books, to visit the cathedral, to become part of Paris life.

In a week he was on the southbound train to Fontainebleau, and in about an hour he was there—in the famous old town in the heart of the Fontainebleau forest. The great palace, where the kings of France had lived when they came to the forest to hunt, was built around four rectangles and stood on the edge of a lake. Around it spread green lawns and flower gardens. The town lay to the west of the palace. Its houses and buildings were prim, three and four stories high, often with hipped roofs.

Aaron and the other young men at the Fontainebleau School of Music for Americans roomed with families in the town. The girls lived in the palace. In a long, wide wing of the palace on the edge of the lake, the students attended classes and ate their meals.

The teachers were from the Paris Conservatory—the best. All summer Aaron Copland would study composing, scoring, and other technical problems of music with them.

First time in a music class.

Now he had classmates to discuss his assignments with. The talking they did together was inspiring and helpful. There really ought to be a school in New York like the one at Fontainebleau, Aaron thought.

They talked after class—or while they strolled through the stone corridors of the palace looking at art treasures—or hanging out a window looking at the green lawns and flower gardens—or at mealtime.

At luncheon Djina Ostrowska usually sat next to Aaron. She was somewhat older than the other students and studying the harp. One day she began to enthuse about one of her teachers, Nadia Boulanger.

"Come and hear her give a talk on harmony, Aaron," she suggested.

"No, thank you. I've had all the harmony I can stand for a while."

"But please come and hear Mademoiselle Boulanger teach."

"Mademoiselle. A woman composer? The world has never produced a first-rate woman composer."

"Aaron Copland, I could hate you for that, but I won't. I shall just make you go."

And she did. She took him by the arm and dragged him to the class.

Mlle. Boulanger was slender and dignified, a very plain person, with a sensitive, delicate face. She had a high forehead and wore rimless glasses clipped to her straight nose. She lived with music around the clock. In the daytime she taught, practiced, and studied, and in the evening she went to a concert.

The first time Aaron Copland went to Mlle. Boulanger's class she was explaining the harmonies in *Boris Godunov*. The first opera he had ever heard! And Mlle. Boulanger proved to be so alive—she could make her subject so clear—that he forgot everything else while she was speaking.

"I suspected that I had found my teacher," he said afterward.

Suspected? In his heart he knew he had discovered one of the greatest teachers in Europe. What good fortune that she had come to Fontainebleau for the summer! Her permanent studio was in Paris. Perhaps when he returned to Paris, he could study with her there.

Fontainebleau held still another experience for him. In September the students gave a recital to show the public how well they had done. Aaron played his piano composition, "Le Chat et la Souris." It went well. As he left the stage, feeling excited and thrilled at having performed his own work before a French audience, a man approached him.

"Mr. Copland, I am Jacques Durand, a music publisher." Durand was Debussy's publisher! "I liked your piece," Mr. Durand said. "Is it published?"

Copland told him it was not. Then, Durand went on, would Copland come to see him in Paris so that they could talk about publishing it?

"Yes," Aaron Copland replied, pretending to great calm. He'd be glad to.

When the course ended at Fontainebleau, Aaron boarded the train for Paris. The first order of business was to call on Jacques Durand, and Durand bought his piece for the marvelous sum of $25.00.

The next task was to find a place for himself and Harold Clurman to live. After a little hunting he found a tiny apartment of two rooms in the heart of Montparnasse, and he rented a cheap upright piano at once.

"We have a place at 207 Boulevard Raspail, across the street from the Café du Dôme," he wrote to Clurman who was still in America, but ready to start for France.

Then Aaron Copland called upon Mlle. Boulanger at 36 Rue Ballu. He was going to ask—plead—beg—that she accept him as a student of composition.

He felt a little shaky when he rang her bell and was

ushered into her studio. But the gentle and sympathetic teacher smiled in a kindly way when she came into the room. She was glad to see Aaron Copland, remembering his work from Fontainebleau. Yes, yes, indeed, she would be glad to have him as a student.

He floated through the air all the way back to the tiny apartment in Montparnasse.

7. Big Goal

By the time Harold Clurman reached Paris, Aaron Copland had plenty to tell him—about his music lessons—about Mlle. Boulanger—more about his music lessons—and more about Mlle. Boulanger.

"She has a consuming love of music," he said. "She knows how to inspire a pupil with confidence in his own creative powers. She knows everything about music, absolutely everything. You know, she was born right here in Paris, and she is half French and half Russian."

Clurman knew without being told that Mlle.

Boulanger was a fine teacher. He could hear the result in Aaron's playing. Aaron spent as many hours at his piano as Harold did in classes at the university.

When they weren't practicing and studying they explored Paris together. They prowled through all the museums and went to as many concerts as they could. Aaron's French grew more natural every day. He seemed to get it by osmosis.

Right in Montparnasse Harold and Aaron found their most wonderful friendships. Just a five-minute walk from their apartment there was a book shop like no other in the world. The sign across the top of the glass fronts said SHAKESPEARE AND COMPANY. The owner, Sylvia Beach, sold and rented books in English. Everybody—artists, novelists, actors, musicians, tourists, students—came to Sylvia Beach's book shop like rabbits to a carrot bin. They came to browse among the shelves and tables full of books and magazines illuminated by soft yellow lamp light. Her shop was a gathering place for young talent. Aaron Copland met James Joyce and Ernest Hemingway there, and he met an intense young man named George Antheil, a pianist-composer.

What stimulating company they all were! Sometimes they sat at tiny tables on the sidewalk in front of a nearby café, drinking little cups of strong coffee, discussing the new poetry, music, books, politics. Often when Aaron and Harold went to a concert, these same young talents were sprinkled through the audience.

Audiences there baffled Aaron Copland at first. Sometimes they hissed or booed. Parisians had fierce feelings about the radical new music—for and against. Riots even broke out at George Antheil's concerts, because he insisted on playing the young, daring composers, including himself. Those who liked the music would applaud and shout. Those who hated it would boo. Then fists would fly. George Antheil played right on.

Aaron Copland loved people, even when they behaved badly. No sooner had he learned his way around Paris than he was helping others to know the city. He especially liked to encourage anyone who seemed to have talent, drawing them into his circle of friends, introducing them to anyone he knew who had the kind of influence he needed. Soon he was known as the most generous man around.

"Weren't you ever jealous of anyone?" he was asked one day.

"When I first went to Paris I was jealous of Antheil's piano-playing," he admitted. "It was so brilliant; he could demonstrate so well what he wanted to do."

His own progress with Mlle. Boulanger was amazing enough. He was composing better and better music. His teacher encouraged him to try different forms. He wrote four motets—pieces for a mixed chorus to sing. Then he tried a piece for string quartet, and "Passacaglia," which is a theme and variations for piano.

The world of music in Paris was beginning to hear works by Copland, through Nadia Boulanger's help. A chorus sang his motets one fall; and the Independent Musical Society performed his "Passacaglia."

His most ambitious composition at that time was a ballet, a piece in which dancers act out the meaning or story. He and Clurman had been to a horror movie about vampires, and when they emerged from the theater Aaron Copland was grinning widely. The movie had given him an idea for a piece of music. At first he wrote a group of piano selections to project the horror mood. When Mlle. Boulanger heard them, she advised him to expand them into a ballet. First he developed the eerie procession called "Cortège Macabre" for piano and two harps. Two years later he completed a ballet, for dancers and full orchestra, calling it *Grohg*. Harold Clurman had written the script for it.

Each week and month—three years in all—that he spent in Paris added to his ability. His growth as an artist showed clearly in his letters home, and his family sent him money to remain longer.

"Let's make every minute count," he and Clurman agreed. During the summers they visited other countries and cities in Europe. Munich in Germany had music festivals that they must not miss. And Vienna in Austria was another city full of musical activity.

One evening they stopped in a café in Vienna to listen to the dance orchestra there. Suddenly Aaron realized, "I am listening to American jazz."

Ever since World War I American jazz had been popular in Europe. People—especially young people—listened to it and danced to it almost everywhere. Jazz was native American music. Jazz rhythm was different, like no other music. It was syncopation. It was contagious. From the moment that Aaron Copland began to analyze jazz, jazz began to influence him.

Vacation ended. He and Clurman returned to Paris, and his thoughts about jazz were lost for the time being.

Each fall when they returned they had to find a new place to live. For their third winter, they knocked at the door of 66 Boulevard Pasteur, not far from their old address in Montparnasse, because they had heard there were rooms for rent.

"Come in, Messieurs," said the man of the family. He was a justice in one of the French courts, they found out. He and his wife were glad to have the students with them, but something had to be faced squarely because the young men were Americans.

"You see, we are mulattoes. Do you have any racial prejudice?"

"Oh, no!" Aaron and Harold burst forth at once, and they meant it.

It was to their own good fortune, for their third winter in Paris was the most amiable of all. The judge and his wife gave them complete privacy to study and work.

They were both reaching the point where they had gained about as much as they could from studying abroad. Aaron Copland was twenty-three years old. It was time to begin his career.

"What do you really hope to do?" Clurman asked him one day. "What is your big goal?"

"I want to write music that will express the present day," Copland told him. "I want to find the musical equivalent for our contemporary tempo and activity."

He did not belong to the romantic past. He belonged to the present and the future—along with men like Antheil and Prokofiev.

Aaron Copland understood the history of music by then. The romantic music of the last century had been due mostly to German influence. For a long time German composers had set the styles, and they were great composers. But now the strong influences were French and Russian. Well, his parents were Russian, and he had come to France to learn all he could. But he *felt* American. He wanted to create truly American music.

He wanted America to become an influence in the music of the world.

During his three years in Paris, one of the most glamorous men in the music life of the city was Serge Koussevitzky, the conductor. Koussevitzky had been born in Russia to a poor family. But he was so gifted that by the time he was seventeen he was a member of the orchestra in the Imperial Theatre in Moscow. After that there was no stopping him. He was in his forties when the Russian Revolution broke out and he had to flee to Paris.

Koussevitzky was the toast of the town when Aaron Copland was there. At the Paris Opera Koussevitzky gave four symphony concerts each fall and four each spring, mostly the newest music. Aaron Copland was usually up in the gallery somewhere listening to them. He realized quickly that Koussevitzky lived, breathed, ate, and slept music, that it was his whole life. And so, naturally, his concerts were the finest that an audience could hope for.

"I, too, want to live, breathe, eat, and sleep music," Copland decided. "It has to be my whole life. That is how to achieve excellence."

"Mr. Koussevitzky is going to America," Mlle. Boulanger told him one day. "He will conduct the Boston Symphony Orchestra."

That meant he would be able to hear the conductor when he went home!

Mlle. Boulanger had more exciting news than that. "I am taking you to meet him," she said.

Nadia Boulanger had so much confidence in Aaron Copland that she had asked the conductor to look at some of his compositions.

Together they went to Mr. Koussevitzky's apartment on the other side of the Seine in an expensive part of town. When they were shown into the drawing room, Aaron Copland discovered that several others had been invited too. Including Prokofiev! Aaron began to feel terribly young.

But as soon as Mr. and Mrs. Koussevitzky entered the room, all was well. The conductor showed so much interest in young composers in general, and Copland in particular, that Aaron quickly felt like himself again. Mr. Koussevitzky was a tall, husky man with a handsome face and dreaming eyes. He was warm and—well—loving. He asked Copland about his studies and then told him to play something of his own.

At Mlle. Boulanger's suggestion Copland had brought along a piano piece from his ballet *Grohg*. After he had played it, a ripple of applause went around the room. Mr. Koussevitzky nodded approvingly.

"I like it," he said. "I shall perform it next season in Boston."

Aaron's mouth was dry as dust, and his knees felt weak as he rose from the piano bench and found his way back to his chair. He heard Mr. Prokofiev remark that there was one section, repetitious in the bass part, that he hadn't liked. But, of course, Aaron hadn't thought his ballet was perfect.

As he and Mlle. Boulanger left the gathering, Aaron Copland sensed his teacher's deep joy. But he didn't realize how truly deep it was until a few days later.

"I am going to America myself," she told him, "to appear as organ soloist with the Boston Symphony and the New York Symphony. I want to present a new work by an American composer. Will you write such a work for me?"

Would he! *Could* he? Mlle. Boulanger believed that he could. Therefore, he must believe in himself. She was giving him his chance to make his debut in America.

Since Mlle. Boulanger was an organist, a piece written for her must be planned around the organ. He began at once to jot down ideas, to make an outline. It would be an organ symphony for solo organ with the orchestra in the background. He decided on the symphony form, which is just about the same as the sonata, except that it is for the whole orchestra.

He always composed sitting at the piano, trying out the sound of his ideas, humming and singing as he worked. His roommate, Harold Clurman, believed in him just as much as his teacher. He left Aaron to himself as much as possible.

They were planning to return home in the spring, and Copland could not possibly complete his organ symphony before then. But he must not expect to. Rushing this composition would be a terrible mistake.

As his three years in Paris drew to an end, his feelings became terribly mixed up. Paris seemed like home. He had formed many true friendships there. But he longed to see his family, too—and Brooklyn—and Manhattan. He wanted to have long talks with John Kober and Aaron Schaffer. Above all else, he must show Mr. Goldmark how far he had developed.

The time of departure drew closer—one more concert, one more visit to Sylvia Beach's book store, one more stroll along the Seine, one more argument about new music at a little sidewalk table. Paris friends began to look at him as though he were about to die.

Mlle. Boulanger cheered them all by giving him a *bon voyage* party in her studio. For the high point of the afternoon, Aaron Copland and Nadia Boulanger played a piano duet—something by Copland.

In June, 1924, he and Harold Clurman at last boarded their ship. They stood at the rail together watching France disappear from view.

France had changed him completely, Aaron Copland realized. France had made him over into what he truly wanted to be—a composer.

8. *Jazz, Jazz, Jazz!*

Gone three years! He headed straight for a big family gathering at home. But not in the store, as for his *bar mitzvah,* and not up over the store. His parents had retired to an apartment in President Street, Brooklyn. Absolutely everyone was there to greet him: married brothers and sisters, uncles, aunts, nieces, nephews—filling the place with happy gasps. "Oh!" said each one as he arrived and greeted the homecomer. Aaron seemed taller, and he probably was. And he was slender and dignified, stylish and genteel. "My good-

ness!" "Welcome home, Aaron. I mean, *Mr. Copland.*"
His parents glowed and beamed. Mama wiped her
eyes every once in a while, and Papa blew his nose
when it wasn't necessary.

"What are your plans, Aaron?" was the standard
question.

He was twenty-four years old, and he had decided
that he must begin to support himself.

He told family and friends about the marvelous assignment that Mlle. Boulanger had given him.

"I'll find a summer job somewhere first and finish
my organ symphony. And in the fall I shall open a
studio in New York and advertise for piano students."

After the family reunion he looked up his old teacher,
Mr. Rubin Goldmark.

"There is to be a music school here in New York,"
Mr. Goldmark told him. "The Juilliard School of Music
opens this year, and I am head of the department of
composition." That meant classes where students could
talk over their assignments with one another. Aaron
was delighted. He had been doing that very thing at
Fontainebleau and it had helped him tremendously.

A job playing with a trio in a summer hotel in Milford, Pennsylvania, solved his financial situation for
the time being. Milford is in the eastern part of the
state, very near the Delaware River. He had gone to
camp in that region as a boy.

He couldn't very well drive the summer guests crazy with his practicing and composing, but there was a motion picture house in town. It had a piano. Aaron Copland charmed the owner into letting him work there when there wasn't any picture showing, usually between the matinee and night show.

All that summer, in the empty theater, he sat at the piano working, several hours every day. At last, one afternoon toward the end of September, he stopped, worn out and elated. He had never felt so happy! In his hands he held a stack of manuscript pages that he himself had written. The Symphony for Organ and Orchestra was complete.

Or was it? He was just as afraid as he was happy—afraid that his teacher would not be satisfied with it. There was only one way to find out—mail it to her in Paris. He did.

Then he returned to New York City to open a studio at 135 West 74th Street—to wait for Mlle. Boulanger's reply—and for piano students. Very few people had ever heard of Aaron Copland, and nobody came knocking at his studio door for lessons. But he did hear from Mlle. Boulanger.

"I can't tell you my joy—the work is so brilliant, so full of music," her letter began. "I am writing by the same mail to Dr. Damrosch to tell him how happy I am to play the work in New York—(I think also in Boston and afterwards, I hope in Paris)——"

She did make some suggestions for improving the second movement, but her happiness showed through the whole letter. If Nadia Boulanger liked it, Mr. Copland, composer, didn't care a great deal what anyone else thought. He really didn't.

"I am sailing December twenty-seventh," she wrote later.

Aaron Copland and Harold Clurman looked after her when she reached New York. They escorted her around, showed her the sights of the city. Of course, she wanted to see where the theaters and concert halls were. So they walked with her up Broadway—the Great White Way—at night when all the electric signs were blinking and blazing. How did she like it, they wanted to know.

"It is extra-*ordinaire!*" she said in her mixture of French and English.

Her concert with Walter Damrosch and the New York Symphony Orchestra took place at Aeolian Hall on January 11, 1925. Harris and Sarah Copland came to New York for it, sitting in a box with their composer-son.

Out came the orchestra. When its members were settled and tuned up, the soloist and conductor walked

out, bowed, and took their places—Mlle. Nadia Boulanger high on the bench of the organ. But Aaron's
piece did not occur until the second half of the program. He had to wait through the first half and through
an intermission that seemed to last forever. Then,
finally . . . the orchestra, Mlle. Boulanger, and the
conductor came back.

This was Aaron Copland's debut, the first performance of his first major work. He listened almost without
breathing as the orchestra and organist played his
Organ Symphony. What a fine artist Nadia Boulanger
was. What a generous teacher to give him this opportunity.

The music startled the audience because it was full
of modern effects. Once or twice there was laughter.
But at the end the audience applauded loudly. Mr. and
Mrs. Copland nodded to each other happily. Then Dr.
Damrosch, who was so conservative, did something
that conductors seldom do. He spoke to the audience.

"Ladies and gentlemen! It seems evident that when
the gifted young American who wrote this symphony
can compose at the age of twenty-four a work like this
one, in five years he will be ready to commit murder."

The audience laughed, and so did the amiable young
composer up in the box. He certainly did intend to
commit murder before he was through. Just wait! Just
wait!

The reviews in the papers were mixed—some pro, some con. The New York *Post* called the Organ Symphony "spasmodic and boisterous . . . an experiment in music." "This young American speaks in the tongue of the ultra-moderns," said *The New York Times.* "The work discloses the existence of a real talent," said the New York *Sun.*

Dr. Damrosch in his remarks had been referring to the fact that the Organ Symphony was full of the new harmonies and methods—and jazz influences. Ever since that day in a Vienna café, when Copland had paused to think about jazz, it had been fermenting in his mind. He was living in a jazz age. So was everyone else. If he bought an ice cream soda, he heard jazz. If he went to a restaurant where there was dancing, he heard jazz. He heard it in the movies, on the radio, everywhere. Jazz was influencing everybody. Naturally, it would influence composers who were particularly sensitive to music of every kind.

Composers in other countries used their *native* music as a basis for their ideas. Jazz was native American. Therefore, he intended to use jazz ideas in writing serious music.

Copland had been studying jazz bands. The drums were the center. Around the drums sat the wood-wind and brass instruments—clarinets, saxophones, trumpets, trombones. No violins or fiddles; sometimes a piano.

The drums were important because rhythm was the most important factor in jazz—an off-beat rhythm.

His use of jazz in writing serious music put him way ahead of his times. That was why Dr. Damrosch had said what he did.

He was much too far ahead for Boston. When Nadia Boulanger played his Organ Symphony there one month later, with the Boston Symphony Orchestra and Mr. Koussevitzky, some people in the audience actually booed. They just weren't ready for such radical ideas. The Boston *Post* called Copland's music "barbaric."

But those who knew music in a professional way were ready, most of all Mr. Koussevitzky. Thanks to his influence, the League of Composers gave Copland a commission to write a new piece that Mr. Koussevitzky would conduct the following winter. The Organ Symphony was only a start. He wanted Copland to go on striving and not let one success go to his head.

Aaron Copland had no intention of letting it go to his head. He was too sensible a person for that. He had already made up his mind to live, breathe, eat, and sleep music—his music—and he would work like a beaver all spring and summer on this new commission. All he needed was a piano, music paper, and pencils—and a peaceful place to work. This soon presented itself, when the music critic, Paul Rosenfeld, told him about the MacDowell Colony in New Hampshire.

In their own way, music critics are as special as composers, because they have to know so much about music in order to judge and criticize it intelligently. Paul Rosenfeld took particular interest in young composers, and he went way out on a limb in his books and magazine articles to give them a boost when he thought they were good. He liked Copland's music very much indeed and made a point to meet him personally.

"Have you ever heard of the MacDowell Colony?" Mr. Rosenfeld said one day.

More than fifteen years ago, the widow of Edward MacDowell had converted their farm and woodlands into a place where artists could work in peace and quiet—as a memorial for her composer-husband. Each composer, writer, or painter had a cottage of his own, somewhere off by itself. Some cottages were made of logs, some of fieldstone, and each had a fireplace for chilly days. After working by himself all day, the artist could stroll along woodland paths to the community house, Colony Hall, to have dinner and spend the evening enjoying the company of other creative people.

Aaron Copland spent all of July and August in one of the cottages amidst pine and spruce and birch trees, and—most important—in peaceful solitude.

His imagination was like a river in flood all that summer. Inspired, keyed up, his pencil flew over the lines on the music paper. One piece for Koussevitzky? He could do more than that. Now was the time! During these lovely weeks in the New Hampshire hills, he wrote two other works for choruses to sing.

By the time he returned to New York, he had a whole stack of work, and his assignment for the League of Composers was finished. He called it Music for the Theatre, and it was for a symphony orchestra.

The opening tones of Music for the Theatre are a short fanfare of drums as in a jazz band, then a solo trumpet sounds—again like a jazz band opening—holding a long tone until it finally moves into the melody. Soon it is joined by the violins. Then a wood wind, the oboe, plays the second melody. The piece is gentle at first, and gradually the whole orchestra combines the two melodies or themes with increasing power. The music rises to a high peak, then drops back, completing the first part.

The second part is a dance, full of tricky rhythms. The third he called an interlude. It is slow and appealing, in a blue, searching mood, that seems, at least in feeling, like something by Debussy. The fourth he called burlesque—full of syncopation. Now and again the low bassoon sounds like a clown or a dancing bear. Fifth is the epilogue, the wrap-up. In it Aaron Copland brings together his beginning ideas, and the piece ends quietly and gently.

What kind of music is this?

"Symphonic jazz," said Mr. Copland.

Conductor Koussevitzky agreed, and he was delighted when he saw it. The Boston Symphony Orchestra played Music for the Theatre on November 20, 1925, in Boston and a few days later in New York. This time the reviews were much more favorable.

"He speaks as one with authority in his music, not as a follower of fashions or schools," said the Boston *Globe*.

Aaron Copland was so full of joy and hope and happiness, he felt as though he would burst.

"You must keep on!" Mr. Koussevitzky insisted. "Do you have enough money to live on?" He always worried that way about young talent.

Yes, Copland had enough, because the John Simon Guggenheim Memorial Foundation had just given him a fellowship. The foundation was brand-new, and Copland was the first composer to receive a grant of money.

"I shall keep on," he promised. "I am so full of ideas I can't stop. Next I shall write a piano concerto." He started it at once.

He was certainly living, breathing, eating, sleeping music—and dreaming and talking it too. He had plenty of musical friends by now who talked music on his level. And there was still his big family who always wanted to hear from him—and his old friend Harold Clurman.

"Let's go back to Paris," said Clurman one day.

Aaron Copland agreed, because he could make his grant money stretch further over there. In addition, whenever an orchestra played his music, he received a fee, or royalty. But there weren't enough of those yet.

In Paris they could pay their respects to Mlle. Boulanger—and look up other old friends.

So they set out that same spring of 1926, and Aaron Copland took his unfinished piano concerto with him.

They found George Antheil very much there—and a success.

"My violin sonata received fine reviews," he told them.

His *Ballet Mécanique* was almost completed. "It is too difficult for any human being to play, and so I am using player pianos along with the orchestra," he explained. "This is a mechanical age, and that is what my ballet will express. This is also the age of the airplane; thus, I shall use two airplane propellers for musical instruments."

Most important to Aaron Copland, though, was his visit with Mlle. Boulanger. She gave him just the kind of encouragement he needed. And at one of her social gatherings he made a new and important friend, Roger Sessions.

Sessions was only four years older than he, and also from Brooklyn. He was a composer who taught music at Smith College, in Northampton, Massachusetts. Copland and Sessions had long discussions about American music. American composers needed more encouragement, they agreed. And good music should be made available to everybody, not just the select few who could afford expensive concert tickets. They promised each other to meet again once they were back in the United States.

Just being in Paris gave Aaron Copland a special kind of lift.

"I must return to Paris as often as I can," he decided. "It is like a second home to me."

Back in his first home, New York, after six months abroad, he took his new Concerto for Piano and Orchestra to Mr. Koussevitzky. By then the great conductor had become as much of an idol in Boston and New York as he had once been in Paris. When he premiered a piece, everyone took notice.

He premiered the Piano Concerto in January, 1927, and Aaron Copland appeared as the soloist, playing the piano part himself. His mother and father made the long journey to Boston, once more to watch their composer-son upon the stage with the most outstanding symphony orchestra in America.

Aaron Copland had again written symphonic jazz.

The Piano Concerto is in two parts. The first begins with the trumpet and a brief stint from the orchestra. Then the piano alone, softly and gently at first, building and growing stronger. Back comes the orchestra, and piano and orchestra build together. The piece becomes louder, more compelling, with mighty sounds from the brasses. The second part is faster, jazzier, and works up to a tremendous and powerful ending. No need for a wrap-up here. That is *it*.

Boston had once turned thumbs down on his Organ Symphony. This time the Boston audience thundered applause. The reviews next day were better than they had ever been—well, most of the reviews. Some people are never ready for new ideas.

The critic writing for the Boston *Globe* said, "No music . . . in the past fifteen seasons has created so great a sensation." Others called it scandalous, criticized him for using saxophones too much.

But most of them admitted that Aaron Copland was on his way to becoming a great composer.

9. More Music for More People

Aaron Copland was now part of the musical fellowship. He knew composers, teachers, conductors, American and foreign, and how they felt about things. Because he was beginning to have so much influence, he continued to meet more and more of them.

Carlos Chávez of Mexico was one. Chávez was only about a year older than Copland, still in his twenties, and already the most important composer in *his* country. Paul Rosenfeld thought his music was terrific and said so in his articles. Naturally, when Chávez came to New York City to live and study for a while, he and Aaron Copland were bound to meet.

Chávez and his mother had a tiny apartment in the Greenwich Village section of town, and they invited Copland to dinner. That was their first real chance to get acquainted.

Señora Chávez knew no English, but she did know how to make the visitor feel welcome. With smiles and gestures, her dark eyes sparkling, she showed him where to sit and then served a typical Mexican meal. And she had only one gas burner to cook it on!

"I feel as though I am in the heart of Mexico," Copland decided.

Chávez had dark and flashing eyes, too; his hair was jet black, his face sensitive and squarish. He had not yet completely mastered English, and Copland knew no Spanish, but they managed to communicate.

Mr. Chávez had a wife, he learned, and two children, four-year-old Anita and two-year-old Augustin. Mrs. Chávez had stayed at home because the children were too young to travel.

Mr. Copland must come to Mexico, Mr. Chávez insisted. Aaron Copland promised he would some day.

The two young composers agreed on many things. Both wanted to make more good music available to people. Both wanted to find new ways to help people understand good music. Mr. Chávez was working to create the Symphony Orchestra of Mexico. He would be its conductor, and he would see to it that new composers got a chance to be heard.

Everybody needed more musical opportunities. Everyone should have the chance to keep up with new works of music just the way they did with new books.

"I must study Spanish," Aaron Copland said to himself after his visit with Carlos Chávez. "He is one of the most valuable musical friendships I have ever made. I must learn to communicate with him better."

He began to discuss musical opportunities with Roger Sessions, who had just returned from Paris.

"Music needs more listeners," they agreed.

Composers trying to create native American music especially needed more listeners.

Since Copland was now lecturing at the New School for Social Research in New York City, he decided to create an opportunity there. He planned a concert of modern music. It was so successful that the school agreed to hold more concerts of new music. Paul Rosenfeld had recommended Aaron Copland for the post at the school, and he was particularly happy about the results.

Aaron Copland told Roger Sessions about those programs. "Arranging concerts isn't hard," he said with excitement. "The more concerts there are, the more composers and people can meet each other."

Soon they were planning a series known as the Copland-Sessions Concerts. Every winter for the next four years, they put on programs of music by new young composers. Interested wealthy persons put up the money. There were several programs each winter at this New York theater or that. A small but devoted public attended them. The Copland-Sessions Concerts did as much as anything else to help make modern American music become better known and better understood.

Mr. Copland's current studio was on West 78th Street. It was just a great big room with a high ceiling. His possessions were: a piano, a couple of chairs and a desk, and some shelves for his books. There he went on with his explorations in music, searching always for new ways to be freshly inventive.

His works were winning more and more attention from conductors. During the summer of 1928 he journeyed to California to play his Piano Concerto at the Hollywood Bowl. One day the following winter the postman brought him some happy news.

The Symphony Orchestra of Mexico, Carlos Chávez, conductor, had played his Music for the Theatre in

Mexico City. The audience had loved it, and so had the Mexican critics.

"I must really try to take a trip to Mexico," Aaron Copland said to himself.

But there were so many other things to do. He was returning to Paris for the summer of 1929 to arrange a concert there of young American composers, so that Europe would know what Americans were doing.

When he came home from Paris, he still could not manage a trip to Mexico, because the bottom had just about dropped out of American prosperity. The stock market crashed in October, 1929. A depression had been developing for some time all over the country. Cotton crops in the south had not sold. Businesses and factories reduced their staffs. Some failed altogether. More people were unemployed, and so they could afford to buy less. Sales in stores fell off. That meant prices had to be reduced, which in turn meant less profits. Then more people had to be laid off, and so on down.

Why? Aaron Copland didn't really understand economics. He had been so engrossed in his music that he hadn't stopped to think about other matters. Commissions for new pieces had always seemed to come his way. He had engagements to play his own works. Awards helped. Wealthy music lovers helped.

Now suddenly the world had changed. He was receiving almost no engagements and commissions. Along with everyone else he felt the pinch. His teaching post at the New School continued through the winter, and that was lucky. But at the end of the term he wondered how long his money would hold out. What if he couldn't pay the rent on his studio? If he had no studio, where could he keep his piano? Without his piano he would be absolutely lost.

He still had his initiative. The RCA-Victor Company had offered an award of $25,000 to the composer submitting the best symphonic piece. He had been working on a new piece to send in to the contest, called Symphonic Ode, but he knew it wouldn't be ready in time. Instead, he took three portions from his ballet, *Grohg*, and made them into a Dance Symphony. He got it in to the judges at just about the last minute. Nobody won the whole prize. But the judges gave $5,000 each to five different contestants, including Aaron Copland. Phew! That money would carry him for a long time.

And then a friend rescued him from the sweltering hot city for the summer.

"Come to Yaddo," was the suggestion of Mrs. Elizabeth Ames, its director. She knew him—and his music.

Yaddo was a retreat for artists outside Saratoga Springs, New York. It had been the home of Mr. and

Mrs. Spencer Trask—acres and acres of woodland with footpaths along lakes and through flowering gardens. In their huge old house with its many rooms and fireplaces and dining hall, Mr. and Mrs. Trask had always loved to entertain summertime guests—especially writers, artists, and composers. Long ago, their four-year-old daughter had named the place Yaddo for shadow, because she liked words that made poetry. "Yaddo, shadow, shadow, yaddo," she had said. When Mr. Trask died, Mrs. Trask made the estate into a summer place for artists in his memory.

There for the whole summer Aaron Copland worked on his newest composition, Piano Variations. Or he strolled through the woods dreaming of another symphony, of ballets, and even of opera.

In the evening he and the other guests gathered in the library or on the lawn—to gab and talk of art and people. They listened with keen interest when he told them he wanted to bring more music to more people. By the end of his stay, he felt sure that something important to music would happen at Yaddo. And eventually it did, due to his influence. Two years later the first music festival at Yaddo took place, and both Aaron Copland and George Antheil were there to play their own works.

Copland went on discovering new ways by which music reached people. When he turned on the radio and heard Walter Damrosch conducting a music appreciation hour for school children, he realized how important radio was. Stations had even begun to broadcast on a nation-wide hookup. On April 2, 1932, the Philadelphia Orchestra broadcast his Music for the Theatre—to the entire country! Radio was a terrific medium.

He knew—he felt—he made up his mind—that some day he would write music for every medium that reached people: the phonograph, the theater, the movies, radio.

For all his musical life he campaigned for good music in every way that he could—as though music were running for President.

10. *Mexico at Last*

His friend, Carlos Chávez, was doing the same thing in Mexico. The founder and conductor of the Symphony Orchestra of Mexico was director of the National Conservatory of Music there as well. Progressive and with an eye on the future, he often played Aaron Copland's compositions on his programs. Now he wanted to have an all-Copland program, and he wanted Mr. Copland to come to Mexico City to appear in person.

Mexico! Copland had been tempted many times—

whenever he received a letter from Chávez, whenever he wrote one to his friend, he wanted to see the country he had heard so much about.

Mexico was said to be full of brilliant sunshine and colors. And it was vast, three and a half times bigger than France, one fourth the size of the United States. Life was said to move at a slower pace. It might prove to be a peaceful place to write music.

"I think I shall spend the entire winter there," he decided, and began at once to take Spanish lessons.

He wrote a long letter to Mr. Chávez accepting the invitation. Then he and a companion started out for Texas by car. The beginnings of a second symphony went with him in his brief case, and so did some other ideas that were just starting to ferment.

From the moment he and his friend boarded the train in Texas and started southward to Mexico City, Aaron Copland realized he was discovering a whole world he hadn't known about. Oh, he had been in the southwestern United States before, but *Mexico!*

Brilliant blue sky—white fleecy clouds—sudden showers followed by brilliant blue—dry, cool air because the land was a high plateau—villages of adobe houses—flowers almost everywhere of deep red, yellow, purple, orange—Indians dressed in serapes and big straw hats, riding burros. That was the countryside. The cities were another matter.

Mexico City was more than five hundred miles south of the Texas border, and it was a real thrill.

"Why!" he thought, as he rode in a taxi from the railroad station to his hotel, "Mexico City is as picturesque in its own way as New York or Paris."

The most important boulevard was Paseo de la Reforma. It was six lanes wide, streaming with cars, decorated with trees and statues. Tall office buildings stood along each side.

Mexico City spread out for miles, its houses and buildings had flat roofs, and here and there rose church spires. All around the city were green plains, and in the distance in every direction there were mountains. To the south rose two giant, snow-covered peaks.

As soon as Mr. and Mrs. Chávez knew he had arrived, they arranged a party for him. How at home he felt with Mexican people! Mexican society is both formal and friendly, and since he was a friendly and courteous person everyone he met liked him at once.

He had arrived just barely in time for the concert in the Teatro de Orientación on September 2, 1932. He sat in the audience that evening and listened happily as Mr. Chávez conducted his Music for the Theatre. A gifted young Mexican pianist, Jesús Durón Ruiz, played his Piano Variations.

Mr. Copland was delighted with the performance, and the audience was delighted with Mr. Copland's music. Next day the Mexican papers praised the program and his music. In fact, the concert was so successful that Mr. Chávez held a second one later that month consisting mostly of Copland's music. That time Aaron Copland played his own Variations.

When the concerts were behind them, Mr. Chávez and Mr. Copland could spend some time together, catching up on news about each other, discussing the latest trends in music—sight-seeing in Mexico.

Copland always wrote to his mother and father about new adventures and experiences. So naturally he sent them a letter from Mexico.

"Last Sunday Chávez took me out to a town called Cuernavaca which is about 50 miles from here. . . . In order to get there you have to climb over an enormous mountain and in doing so get a marvelous view of Mexico City and the valley beyond. . . ."

Mr. Chávez's English was just about fluent by then, and that was the language he and Mr. Copland usually used together, although Aaron Copland was getting on well with his Spanish, finding it much easier than French. He spent four months in Mexico, and by the end of that time he had a good working knowledge of the language.

With the help of his new friends he had found a studio on the ground floor of a quiet street near the center of Mexico City. There he went on with his composing. The last two months of his stay he spent in a small villa in a picturesque suburb of Mexico City, called Tlalpan.

He wrote to his family that Mexico City was really a quiet place to work. "People don't run after you here as they do in New York. This is fine for me because I can work so much better that way. My Spanish is improving. I can go into a restaurant now and order a whole meal in Spanish without any difficulty. . . . In general, I lead a very quiet life here and it is quite like living in the country."

But how different a country, with its ancient Indian history going back thousands of years—both Aztec and Mayan—its mixture of Indian and Spanish customs!

During their trips and visits to different parts of Mexico Chávez and Copland talked often about Mexican music.

"I want to see a native Mexican concert music develop," said Mr. Chávez. "I have traveled among the Indians and Spanish, and I have heard many ancient songs that have never been written down. These are the true Mexican music. I have used them and their strange instruments for my musical ideas."

Folk music. German composers had used German folk songs. Russian composers had used Russian folk songs. The same had happened in France, Poland, Hungary. . . . And now Chávez in Mexico.

Why not all of America? There must be thousands of songs—sung by mountain people, cowboys, ranchers, river boatmen, outlaws, Indians, religious groups. This was all genuine American folk music, and it ought to be written down and adapted.

And Mexico was absolutely loaded with folk music.

One night Copland and some friends visited a dance hall in Mexico City called El Salón México. The hall—a long center section, with an ell at each end that gave it the shape of a U—was divided into three parts. At one end the wealthy people danced; in the long center section the middle-class people danced; and at the other end the peasants danced in their bare feet. A sign warned people not to throw cigarettes on the floor so that the dancers would not burn their feet. Wherever the people danced, or however they danced, the music was contagious.

Aaron Copland couldn't forget the place, or the people who enjoyed themselves there. Fragments of the folk melodies kept buzzing around in the back of his mind.

His stay in Mexico finally came to an end, and everybody was sorry.

"Please páy us another visit," Mr. Chávez pleaded.

Some composers were—well—a little on the crazy side. But not Mr. Copland. He was gentle, generous, warmhearted, and easy to get along with. They wanted more of him.

And he had learned to love Mexico and Latin American life.

"I shall come to Mexico again," he promised.

All the way back to New York he thought about Mexico, about Mr. Chávez and his music, and about the folk songs of that colorful country.

11. Music for Children

Home—a studio in New York City in the winter, somewhere in the country during the hot weather—Aaron Copland worked with more verve than ever. But being home also meant having many irons in the fire. He had a long list of commitments, so Mexico was crowded into the background for a while.

In 1935 he began to teach a group of students from the Henry Street Settlement House. The Henry Street project had been founded years before by Lillian Wald to bring nursing service to the people in the slums. It had grown and grown until it even included a music school.

Most of Aaron Copland's students at Henry Street were adults who lived all over town. And since his studio was more central than the school, they came to his studio for class. But even so, he had many conversations with the music director at Henry Street, Miss Grace Spofford. He and she agreed that music could do a lot to brighten life in the slums.

"There isn't enough good music especially for children," she told him. "Have you ever thought of writing music that is easy enough for children to play and sing? Our students want to put on an opera, but adult operas are all too difficult, and they are about subjects that don't interest young people."

Music especially for children!

"The idea is completely attractive," said Mr. Copland.

It was more than that. It was positively inspiring. He would bring children and good music closer together. The world of children was a whole new audience.

A few weeks later he was working on an opera for the students of the Henry Street Music School. A poet friend, Edwin Denby, had written a play or libretto for it, and its title was to be *The Second Hurricane*.

"This will be a play-opera," he decided. He meant that some of the lines would be spoken, some sung.

His friends teased him about it. "Don't you mean an operetta?" one of them laughed.

"No indeed!" said Mr. Copland. "I am writing a serious opera for children to perform."

He planned it so that the entire school could take part. There were six principal characters, four boys and two girls. Then there were two choruses seated in bleachers on opposite sides of the stage. One represented the parents, and the other the high school students. The school orchestra supplied the music.

In the story the six children go aboard an airplane to fly food and medical supplies to some hurricane and flood sufferers. Before they go, the chorus of "parents" protests, advises them to stay home; it's too dangerous. The chorus of "children" sings back that this is what parents always say. "Be careful," sing the parents, and the children sing happily of adventure as they take off.

On the way the plane develops engine trouble. The pilot lands in a desolate place, but has to leave the children and supplies there, while he flies the empty plane on to an airfield where he can have it repaired. While the six principal characters are alone, a second hurricane blows up. The river rises. They are marooned on a high piece of ground and in great danger. At first

they quarrel among themselves because they are ter-
rified. But finally they come to realize that they must
stand together and help one another if they are to
survive.

"Writing for children is one of the most gratifying
things I have ever done," Copland decided when the
first draft of the music for *The Second Hurricane* was
completed. This was just a beginning. He had more
ideas about music for children. The choruses at Henry
Street needed music, and high school orchestras ought
to have their own music, too.

"I am spending the summer in Mexico," he wrote to
Miss Spofford, "and there I shall finish the orchestration for *The Second Hurricane*."

During that summer he was also going to orchestrate
another piece he had been working on, El Salón
México. The folk songs he had heard on his last trip
to Mexico had haunted him until he finally decided
to compose a piece of music that included them.

On this second visit to Mexico he planned to live in
the town of Tlaxcala, fifty miles east of Mexico City.
Tlaxcala is old and quaint, with narrow, unpaved
streets and rows of adobe houses. It is quiet, too, and
out of the way, with clear dry air and cool nights for
sleeping. Since it is only about an hour away from
Mexico City by bus, Aaron Copland could visit Carlos
Chávez from time to time.

After a happy, productive summer, he returned to New York with two finished projects. Rehearsals got under way at Henry Street for the children's opera, and in Mexico City for his El Salón México. For he had agreed to let Mr. Chávez give the first performance of his Mexican composition.

The Second Hurricane had its first performance at the Grand Street Playhouse on April 21, 1937. And because the directors of the school made a benefit out of it, a parade of limousines brought wealthy patrons down from uptown for the performance. Outstanding music critics traveled to the slums to cover the event, too. Most of them praised it, as well as the director, Orson Welles. Just about everyone declared the opera an important step forward in writing music suitable for young people to perform.

Very soon afterward Mr. Copland received a request from the New York High School of Music and Art. Would he consider writing a piece of music for the high school orchestra? He would and he did, calling it An Outdoor Overture.

He was eager to return to Mexico; Mexico was in his blood, and he wanted to be there for the premiere of El Salón México in August, 1937. Setting out for Tlaxcala once more, he carried a new commission—his first opportunity to write for radio. It was for CBS, and he planned to call it simply, Music for Radio. But when CBS finally saw it, they liked it so much that they held a contest so that listeners could pick their own title. The winning title was, "Saga of the Prairie."

When Aaron Copland appeared in Mexico City for rehearsals, he found everyone excited about El Salón México. And no wonder, because it is a bright and delightful piece of music. Snappy, full of folk melodies— some familiar, some strange—it expresses the color and vitality of Mexico.

The Symphony Orchestra played it twice that summer, in the Palacio de Bellas Artes, and it was a tremendous success. One music critic wrote, "For the first time . . . we have heard a folklore composition without European influence. Copland shows us the path to follow. . . ."

The path to follow—to achieve a truly American music—yes, that was what he had been striving for all these years.

After the success of El Salón México, he knew he must have another big try at American folk music. A commission from a dance group called the Ballet Caravan turned the trick.

The Ballet Caravan was new; many of its dancers had trained under the famous Russian-born choreographer, George Balanchine. Its directors were just as interested in developing a truly American style of dancing as Copland was in writing a truly American music. They showed him a scenario, or story-plan for the ballet, written by Lincoln Kirstein. It was the story of Billy the Kid.

Aaron Copland was excited at once. The most popular legends in America were about cowboys and Indians and the Wild West. The most contagious folk songs were cowboy songs. Billy the Kid—the notorious outlaw with so many notches in his gun! By heaven, here was an idea for a ballet. Write it? He'd love it!

The Ballet Caravan people were excited too, because Aaron Copland was becoming as popular and well known as Billy. The combination of the two would have real drawing power.

As a matter of fact, Mr. Copland was becoming so popular that he had to find places to hide during the summer so that he could work. He took the Billy scenario with him to his second home, Paris, to work on it. When he returned, he hid away in the MacDowell Colony to finish it. By September it was ready, and he was in Chicago to be present at rehearsals.

The dancers loved the *Billy the Kid* music so much they were positively air-borne, and they put their whole hearts into learning their steps.

The first scene is in a frontier town, with wooden buildings and a dusty street. The music here is gay and lively. "Git Along, Little Dogies" pops into it every once in a while. Cowboys saunter around practicing their rope tricks. Ladies stroll by in long, full dresses. Mexican women do a hat dance. Then come young Billy and his mother.

Two drunken cowboys begin to tumble about in a fist fight. Guns are drawn. A stray bullet kills Billy's mother. That does it. Billy becomes an avenging killer, a real bad man. "Oh, bury me not on the lone prairie," sighs the orchestra. The posse chase Billy. In a big gun battle they capture him and put him in jail. One of the Mexican girls helps him escape. But the posse find him again and this time they gun him down. A group of women mourn his passing with a slow, sad dance.

When the first performance of *Billy the Kid* took place in Chicago, October, 1938, it wasn't just a success. It was a sensation. The audience cheered and applauded. The Chicago papers praised it to the skies.

The Ballet Caravan went on tour, dancing *Billy the Kid* wherever they went. They reached New York City in May, and the Martin Beck Theater was jammed. *Billy* was the big hit. "An exceedingly accomplished score," said the New York *World Telegram*. The *Times* called it a "perfectly delightful piece of work . . . it opens up new possibilities of theater dancing." The *Brooklyn Daily Eagle*, Aaron Copland's home-town rag, said that *Billy* was "a success from the start . . . colorful . . . cleverly conceived."

Could a composer ask for more? Of course not. Aaron Copland was deeply happy and gratified. He knew he was influencing other young composers to follow in his footsteps. Still the most generous man around, he was taking his turn at helping and encouraging beginners the way Mlle. Boulanger and Serge Koussevitzky had helped and encouraged him. America was finding her place among the music leaders of the world, and he was doing as much as anyone to help bring that about.

"Where are you hiding this summer, Aaron?" his family wanted to know in 1939.

"Woodstock, New York," he told them.

Woodstock is a vacation town where artists of every sort stay. They like it because artists understand one another and realize *why* a painter or writer or composer must not be disturbed while he is working.

In 1939, Woodstock provided a special treat, because Benjamin Britten was spending the summer there, too.

Aaron Copland had met Benjamin Britten just the summer before at a festival of modern music in London. They were both composers, and composers need other composers to talk music with. Very few people know as much about music as those who write it. It is a special kind of language.

Britten was an intense Englishman of twenty-five—

tall, fair, rather gawky. He was so involved in music that he had burst into a torrent of talk on that first meeting in London with the world-famous Copland.

"How long have you been composing?" Copland had asked him.

"Oh," laughed the young man, "my mother tells me I wrote my first original music at five. I don't remember it too well, but I'm sure it goes that far back."

The young man had a quiet kind of charm. He didn't try to impose his personality on the person he was talking to. He just grew on him.

He told Copland he had had a scholarship to the Royal College of Music in London. Copland knew from others that Britten had progressed like a meteor after that. And he knew that Britten, like himself, had written a great deal of music for children and young people—probably more than any other composer of his reputation.

In their free time at Woodstock, New York, they discussed many subjects. Aaron Copland told Britten about his desire to compose motion picture scores, and about a book he had been writing. Books were another way to help people understand music, and he had just finished *What to Listen for in Music*.

Britten told him that conditions were bad in Europe. All the countries were mobilizing armies.

"Let's hope there won't be a war," they agreed.

But by September, 1939, World War II had started. Marching armies were under way, and so were the killings and bombings.

Copland hoped nobody would bomb Paris—the opera, the art museums, the parks, Notre Dame Cathedral, Sylvia Beach's book shop, the Sorbonne where Clurman had studied, Mlle. Boulanger's studio.

Thousands of people had to flee from Europe. Many sought safety in the United States, Mlle. Boulanger among them. She taught at Wellesley and Radcliffe colleges and at the Juilliard School during the war.

Aaron Copland was grateful that American students had the opportunity to study with her. But the idea of war and killing made him deeply unhappy. He hated violence.

Depressed though he felt at times, he knew life must go on. The good things in life must go on too, and music was one of them. Besides, he was a naturally happy person, bubbling with good humor. All he had to do to feel right was to run his fingers over the piano keyboard.

Watching capable artists perform made him feel right, too. One evening he and a friend went to a dance recital by Anna Sokolow. Suddenly his friend leaned over to introduce him to a young man sitting on the other side of him.

"May I present Leonard Bernstein? And this is Mr. Aaron Copland."

"I nearly flipped!" is how Leonard Bernstein describes the meeting.

Bernstein was a Harvard student. He and some other students had come to New York to see Anna Sokolow, because they were all in love with her for the time being. But Aaron Copland! He worshiped Copland's music. Just recently a friend of his at Harvard had taken him to the music shop in Harvard Square and urged him to listen to a recording of Copland's Piano Variations.

"I was overwhelmed by the music," he went on. "I couldn't understand it very well." But he knew it was tremendously original, far-out. He had begun to imagine Copland as something of a prophet who had things to say to the world, an Isaiah with a flowing white beard. He had talked about the Variations so much that one of his professors bought him the sheet music so that he could learn how to play it. Then he had gone around playing it at parties. It was a severe piece, and it shocked people. That made him want to play it all the more—out of pure devilment.

And now here he sat beside the prophet who had written the piece. Only Aaron Copland wasn't an old man with a long white beard. He was a young man in his thirties, with no beard at all.

Aaron Copland listened patiently to the bundle of excitement and tension sitting beside him.

"After the recital, I want you to come back to my studio," said Mr. Copland when he could get a word in edgewise. "It is my birthday, and I am giving a party."

That year Aaron Copland had a floor in a loft building on West 63rd Street, where the New York State Theater at Lincoln Center now stands. There Leonard Bernstein, eager for a career in music, found himself among all sorts of *name* people: composers, at least one novelist whose books he knew well, music critics. Yes, there was Virgil Thomson.

After Mr. Copland had mingled among his guests, he walked over to Leonard Bernstein and said, "Come; let me hear how you play my Variations."

Leonard Bernstein went to the piano and played— brilliantly. In fact, he stayed at the piano for about four hours, playing everything he knew. And that was the beginning of another lifelong friendship. In the years that followed, whenever Leonard Bernstein came down to New York, he visited Aaron Copland. Whenever Copland went to Boston, he visited Bernstein. After Bernstein was graduated from college, Copland did what he could to help him find a job.

Aaron Copland never stopped helping people, especially young composers and musicians with talent. He called the attention of the music world to many who later made it to the top. One of them was David Diamond, a violinist-composer. When he was only nineteen, Diamond had played some of his compositions for Mr. Copland, playing rather badly because he was so nervous. All Mr. Copland said at the time was, "Hmmmm." But later he wrote an article for the magazine, *Modern Music.* In it he said that Diamond was among the most gifted young composers of the decade. "I guess I have not failed him," said Mr. Diamond years later, and he certainly had not. Diamond has written and published a long list of successful compositions—symphonies, string quartets, and other work for orchestra.

By the end of his thirties, Copland himself was moving into place as the number one composer of the United States. This fact was becoming so apparent that at long last even Hollywood found out about him. And producers began to ask him to write scores for motion pictures.

He could sit back and really chuckle at that. The joke was on him—or—wait a minute—maybe the joke was on Hollywood. He managed his own business problems, contracts, royalties, and such. Many of his commissions to write music came to him because he was enterprising. He knew how to go after opportunities in a nice way. Why should he not go after an opportunity in Hollywood, he had thought several years before.

"You'll never break into Hollywood," everyone had told him. "That is a closed corporation."

"We shall see," he had replied.

He saw.

Harold Clurman was working in Hollywood at the time. With encouragement from Clurman he went about Hollywood calling on producers and film composers. He just couldn't seem to connect. "We aren't in the market for anything. We will get in touch with you if we are," they said just about as often as he could bear it.

Then his common sense had asserted itself, and he went on to other things—to writing El Salón México, *The Second Hurricane,* and *Billy the Kid.*

And finally, after the success of the ballet, Hollywood had discovered him! He was to write the musical scores for two major motion pictures.

And then his old friend and sponsor, Serge Koussevitzky, invited him to teach at Tanglewood during the summer of 1940.

For the past three years Koussevitzky and the Boston Symphony had been giving summer concerts, or festivals, in the Berkshire Hills of western Massachusetts. Each summer more and more people flocked to the Berkshire Festivals held just outside of the town of

Lenox. There in a wide expanse of green lawns, stands the big hall called the Music Shed. In the distance rise blue-green mountains, and Lake Mahkeenac is nearby. The festivals became so popular that at last Mr. Koussevitzky and the Boston Symphony started a summer music school there.

Nothing could have pleased Aaron Copland more than to spend a summer working so close to the great Koussevitzky. Copland was named head of the Composition Department and taught there that season and many more afterward. Eventually he became assistant director of the school.

Naturally, a lot of talented young composers came to the school when they heard they could study composition with the noted Aaron Copland. One of the most glamorous of them was the twenty-two-year-old Leonard Bernstein. Koussevitzky had practically adopted him by then, because he saw such a big future for the slender, dark-haired young man. Leonard Bernstein didn't attend any of Aaron Copland's classes, but he often came with a new composition, asking for criticism. Copland gave "Lenny" all the time and attention he could.

Sometimes Copland said, "This is well done." Sometimes he said, "This is poor; let me show you why." But he always said, "Write more. Stick to it."

The first two summers at Tanglewood were happy,

but the third, in 1942, was a mixture of happiness and sorrow. For the United States had entered the war in December, 1941. Thousands of American men were going overseas to fight and die.

12. *The Pulitzer Prize*

Dark days followed. People thought much more about going into the armed forces and working in war factories than about concerts. But music was just as important, though in a different way. Dancers and singers and musicians began to go overseas to entertain troops.

Aaron Copland was more than forty by then. It was too late for him to learn how to be a soldier. But he could write the kind of music America needed.

To him anything American was patriotic: cowboys and Indians, America's great Presidents, her prairies and mountains, roaring factories and subways. Music could express any of these, and eventually he did write music about all of them.

Very shortly after the war started, the conductor Franz Allers said, "Agnes de Mille wants to meet you."

She was an outstanding ballet dancer, and a dance group called the Ballet Russe de Monte Carlo had asked her to create an American ballet for them.

Aaron Copland nodded. He had heard about the dance group, and he had seen Agnes de Mille perform.

"Come with me to her studio, Mr. Copland. She has a scenario all ready, and she insists that you write the music because she considers you the best composer in America."

Aaron Copland flashed his old smile and agreed to go. He discovered that Agnes de Mille was extremely dynamic, full of wit and mischief—and temperament. She believed that ballet could be comical as well as serious, gay or sad, formal or free.

Her studio was a bare room with one chair, a piano and bench, and her bed. Miss de Mille sat on the piano bench, Allers took the chair, and Copland flopped back upon a pile of pillows on the bed.

"Well?"

"The ballet is to be called *Rodeo*," Miss de Mille explained. It was about a cowgirl who tried to do all the

manly things on a ranch—riding, bronco busting, rop-
ing—to win the love of a cowboy. When Miss de Mille
finished describing the rest of the story, nobody said
anything, and she began to feel discouraged.

"Well," she apologized, "it isn't *Hamlet*."

Copland laughed gaily. "Couldn't we do a ballet
about Ellis Island? That I would love to compose."

Agnes de Mille told him where to go in plain English.

Allers was confused and frightened. "What has happened?" he asked. He wanted these two artists to work
together, not quarrel.

"Mr. Copland and I have just reached a basic understanding," said Miss de Mille.

Copland and Agnes de Mille both looked happy,
but Allers still didn't realize that everything was settled, until Miss de Mille said to Aaron Copland, "You'll
get the scenario by post tomorrow. If you like it at all,
come to tea."

As soon as the mailman arrived next morning,
Copland opened the package containing the manuscript and read it right away. It was good! It was very
good! He called Agnes de Mille's number, to make an
appointment.

They went to work the minute he reached her studio,
planning the story-dance minute by minute, step by

step. Only when a composer knows how many minutes and seconds each part will take, can he write his music to fit.

The Ballet Russe de Monte Carlo presented *Rodeo* in the old Metropolitan Opera House in the fall of 1942, and it was another smash hit. *Rodeo* became as popular as *Billy the Kid*.

Copland's next wartime assignment came from André Kostelanetz, who was a guest conductor with the Cincinnati Symphony Orchestra.

"I want to discover what music can do to mirror the magnificent spirit of our country," Kostelanetz had said. Then he asked several composers, Copland among them, to paint musical portraits of great Americans.

Copland chose Abraham Lincoln.

"How can I describe Abraham Lincoln with music?" he pondered. Soon he knew. He would make Abraham Lincoln's own voice the most important instrument in the orchestra. Selecting his favorite passages from Lincoln's speeches and writings, he created background music for them. Thus, when the Cincinnati Symphony performed A Lincoln Portrait, Carl Sandburg read the words of Lincoln while the music accompanied him. Lincoln Portrait has become one of Aaron Copland's best loved and best known compositions.

He still thought deeply of American folk songs, and one summer at Tanglewood he came across a book of old Shaker songs and hymns. The Shakers? They were a small religious group that kept to themselves and believed in living plain, good lives. He browsed through the book, and one song in particular took his fancy: "The Gift to Be Simple." The melody was lovely, full of possibilities. His imagination began to play with it.

"The Gift to Be Simple" kept popping in and out of his mind, as he went on to other things.

The Elizabeth Sprague Coolidge Foundation asked him to write a ballet for the famous dancer, Martha Graham. And so he called on her.

Martha Graham turned out to be a deeply dramatic person. She had a long oval face and jet black hair. Although she was slender and not very tall, she became a power upon a stage the minute she began to dance.

"Dancing must express emotion," she said. "The dancer must be telling the audience something with every movement."

She showed him the scenario, and as he read, "The Gift to Be Simple" popped back into his mind.

Soon they were at work, planning the dancing and music, minute by minute, step by step.

This time the story was charming, about pioneer life in Pennsylvania. The principal dancers were a young bride and groom, about to move into their new farmhouse in the Appalachian hills. They danced to express their joys and their fears and to show their great hopes for the future. Another important dancer was the preacher, or revivalist, in a long black coat and round-brimmed hat. His dancing was full of advice for the bride and groom. He twirled about to warn them not to be wicked. He held his hands high over their heads to give them his blessing. Yet another dancer was a pioneer woman, whose dancing assured the bride and groom and gave them confidence.

"We will call this ballet *Appalachian Spring,*" Martha Graham suggested, and Aaron Copland agreed.

He worked a long time on the music for *Appalachian Spring*—something like a year and a half. He used several musical ideas or melodies in it, but the most important one was "The Gift to Be Simple." He varied it in five different and original ways.

At last, in the spring of 1944, he turned over the completed score to Martha Graham and her group so that they could start rehearsals.

He felt completely weary.

"I must take a vacation before I start my next work," he realized. Paris was impossible during wartime, but he could go to Mexico. Yes, that would be the place to relax and rest.

Rest? Well. . . . The musician in Aaron Copland was never at rest. He had begun to have deep feelings about a piece of pure music, the most difficult he had ever thought about in his whole life—his third symphony. He had explored the possibilities of jazz and folk music; now he must go on to still more experiments. He must strive to be original in another new way.

To make his third symphony as fine as possible, he planned to live in a little known Mexican village named Tepoztlán. There he could give his whole heart and mind to his work. When he wanted to relax he could drive to Mexico City and talk the language of music with Carlos Chávez. Chávez would understand every problem exactly. He would understand just how Aaron Copland was struggling with his composition.

He drove as far as San Antonio, Texas, by car. But no sooner had he settled in his hotel room when shocking news reached him. A telegram from his sister Laurine told him that his mother had died. That meant both parents were gone, since he had already lost his father.

Seizing the phone he called the airline at once. Could he have a seat back to New York? They were sorry. No space. But he must be at his own mother's funeral! The airline people regretted this deeply, but he must realize that there was a war going on. Civilians were just out of luck when it came to last-minute travel reservations.

A telegram and then a long letter to his brothers and sisters explained his predicament. They would understand. He knew they would. Even though he traveled all over the world, he was still very close to his whole family. But this did not help his grief, or the deep hurt that he felt at not being able to go home when he wanted to so badly.

There was nothing to do but continue on to Tepoztlán.

The ancient village sat among mountain peaks and high cliffs. Its streets were narrow, steep, and cobbled. High on a hill, the point of an Aztec pyramid rose above the town, and brilliant red poinsettias grew wild everywhere.

There in the peace and quiet Aaron Copland's sorrow healed. He settled down to work in a rented house with a separate studio. A friendly American in nearby Cuernavaca loaned him a piano. In a few weeks he could look over the music he had written and feel good about it. He was still searching, learning, improving, growing, writing better this year than he ever had before. That was really what mattered most. His third symphony would probably not be done for another year. It would have to take its own time.

He returned to Washington, D.C., in October for the first performance of *Appalachian Spring* in the Coolidge Auditorium of the Library of Congress. Martha Graham and her group danced like the great artists that they were. Inspiring! Gratifying! was how Aaron Copland found it.

"The fullest, loveliest, and most deeply poetical of all his theatre scores," said *The New York Times,* and critics in other newspapers agreed.

The whole music world cocked its head. Audiences in other cities demanded to see a performance of *Appalachian Spring.* Soon it received the award of the Music Critics Circle of New York for the 1944/1945 season.

That wasn't all—not by any means.

Aaron Copland received a phone call from his publisher telling him that he had received the 1945 Pulitzer Prize for Music. He had reached the top!

He began to realize how very far he had come. A long time ago his first piano teacher had told him he was starting too late. "I'll make it up," he had promised. And he certainly had.

Aaron Copland felt only one secret regret. He was sorry that his mother and father had not lived to know this moment. What would they have said? He knew. After kissing and blessing him, they would both have said, "Don't let it go to your head, Aaron."

Which was really the hardest thing in the world to remember, because everybody was congratulating him, making a fuss over him, sending him fan mail, giving him parties. He was beset with people who wanted to meet him.

"If it does go to my head, I'm through," he realized. "It is time to disappear."

He went into hiding in Ridgefield, Connecticut, where nobody would think of looking for him—in a house that he rented from a fellow composer. There he would calm down and work undisturbed on his Third Symphony.

That same year World War II came to an end—to everyone's joy and relief. Soon it would again be possible to go anywhere, live anywhere, hold music festivals in any country in the world.

The festival at Tanglewood that summer was the most exciting and stimulating in years. The big project was the rehearsal and performance of Benjamin Britten's new opera, *Peter Grimes,* commissioned by Koussevitzky.

Benjamin Britten was there in person, and the rising star, Leonard Bernstein, with his energy and high spirits, directed the performance. *Peter Grimes* was performed in a theater that was really a remodeled stable in nearby Richmond, Massachusetts.

Happy, chattering, laughing, music-loving throngs came to see and hear the new opera. What a wonderful way to celebrate the return of peace!

13. *A Very Special Person*

After the weeks of fellowship at Tanglewood—and the throngs that had come to the concerts and perform-ances of *Peter Grimes*—Aaron Copland slipped away to be by himself for a while. He needed to be alone to put the finishing touches on his Third Symphony.

At last, in September, 1946, he could say, "It is done."

There was only one orchestra and one conductor in the world to premiere the Third Symphony as far as Aaron Copland was concerned: the Boston Symphony

Orchestra and Serge Koussevitzky. And since the Koussevitzky Foundation had commissioned the Third, that was how it came to be.

When Mr. Koussevitzky looked over the score, he was profoundly proud of this composer who had made his debut with the Boston Symphony more than twenty years before.

Mr. Copland himself described his Third Symphony this way: "Let the music speak for itself. It contains no folk songs. Any reference to jazz or folk material in this work is purely unconscious." It was pure music, and each listener must react in his own way.

One writer called it "a glorified and expansive hymn —of prayer, of praise, of sorrow, of patriotic sentiment."

His style has "carrying power," wrote Virgil Thomson in the *Herald Tribune*. To him the Third Symphony was "the work of a mature master," one with "dignity and simplicity."

It was certainly a new and splendid high in Aaron Copland's career.

"I shall premiere your Third Symphony in Mexico City in June," Carlos Chávez wrote to him. "Please honor us by conducting it yourself."

How like a homecoming that would be! Of course, Mr. Copland accepted the invitation.

The Third Symphony won the Music Critics Circle Award and the Boston Symphony Merit Award. Today it is played by all the important symphony orchestras of the world, along with many of Mr. Copland's other works.

Audiences want to see him in person, too. Not only is he America's most outstanding composer, but he has a warm and friendly personality. Like the Cheshire cat in *Alice in Wonderland,* his smile stays around long after he has left.

That is why the United States State Department has asked him to make goodwill tours of Latin America on two different occasions. The first was in 1947. For six weeks he traveled from one important city to the next all over South America, conducting orchestras, playing his own works, giving radio talks. Sometimes he spoke in Spanish.

What delighted him was the amount of musical activity he found in the Southern Hemisphere. There were fine symphony orchestras, big audiences, and outstanding composers.

"Music-lovers who imagine that South America is still a musical desert, creatively considered, simply don't know what is going on," he said when he returned.

His trip to the new country of Israel four years later

proved to be another tremendous experience. He played and conducted for audiences there. And he did something that no other composer had done before—he met with thirty of Israel's young composers for nearly a week.

"I want to hear your work," he told them. Listening carefully to each piece, he gave them expert advice and criticism and encouragement. "You are doing fine; keep on," he urged.

In 1960, Charles Munch, the conductor of the Boston Symphony Orchestra who succeeded Koussevitzky, invited Aaron Copland to go on a tour of the Orient as guest conductor. He accepted and conducted the Boston Symphony in Japan, the Philippines, and Australia.

In Japan he became enormously popular. The Japanese people already liked his music, and they loved him for his gentle, courteous manner. He discovered that Japan has adopted western music. It is rapidly replacing the ancient Japanese-style music.

Whenever Aaron Copland goes to London to be guest conductor of the London Symphony Orchestra, he visits with Benjamin Britten at his home in Aldeburgh, on the eastern coast of England. There they can take long walks together along the edge of the North Sea, while the sharp wind burns their cheeks.

Today he enjoys conducting almost as much as composing. But he feels that the most important thing he does is his composing.

He writes music for all the media that reach people. He composed for the movies *The Red Pony* and *The Heiress*. The second one received an Oscar for the best film score of the season 1949/1950.

He even tried his hand at opera, *The Tender Land*, but he wasn't satisfied with the results, and neither were the critics. Opera simply wasn't the best medium for him. His admirers were all glad when he returned to writing concert music.

Benny Goodman premiered his Concerto for Clarinet and String Orchestra. And since then the world has enjoyed Copland's Piano Fantasy, Orchestral Variations, and Emblems for Band. He has collected and arranged a dozen "Old American Songs" so that people can hear them on their record players.

"What is enchanting about Copland is his tenderness, his sustained youthfulness, his curiosity of things new and avant-garde, and his faith in young composers of talent," David Diamond said recently.

Aaron Copland influences listeners with his magazine articles and books on music appreciation. And he influences young composers with his teaching. Many of the up-and-coming young composers in America today have been his students at some time or another.

"Be original," he tells them. "Explore and experiment; write for your own times. America is industrial; make that part of your music. This is a space age; write that into your music, too. And don't forget also to express your innermost thoughts."

On September 14, 1964, Aaron Copland appeared in the East Room of the White House at noon. He and twenty-four other men and five women were to receive a gold decoration from the President of the United States—the Medal of Freedom—the highest honor that the President can bestow. Each person worked in a different field. Among them were the former Secretary of State, Dean Acheson; Walt Disney; T. S. Eliot and Carl Sandburg, poets; John L. Lewis and A. Philip Randolph, labor leaders; the actor and actress, Alfred Lunt and Lynn Fontanne; Edward R. Murrow, the newsman.

When Aaron Copland stepped forward to receive his decoration and shake the President's hand, his award was for being a "leading force in the development of the modern American school of composition."

Long ago he had told Harold Clurman that his big goal was "to write music that will express the present day . . . to find the musical equivalent of our contemporary tempo and activity." He has certainly achieved his goal.

To him a composer is a very special person who speaks a rare language. He must strive to express himself in that language in the finest ways possible.

Chronological List of Representative Works
of Aaron Copland

The Cat and the Mouse (1920), Piano Solo
First performed by the composer at the Salle Gaveau,
Paris, September 23, 1921.
Sheet music published by Boosey and Hawkes, Inc.
Four Motets (1921), for Unaccompanied Mixed Chorus
1. Adagio ma non troppo
2. Allegro (Molto ritmico)
3. Molto Adagio
4. Vivo
First performed by the Paris-American-Gargenville Chorus
conducted by Melville Smith, Fontainebleau School, Fall
of 1924.
In manuscript only
Passacaglia (1922), Piano Solo
First performed by Daniel Ericourt at the Société Musicale
Indépendante, Paris, January, 1923.
Dedicated to Nadia Boulanger
Salabert
Cortège Macabre (1923), for Symphony Orchestra
Later part of the ballet "Grohg"
First performed by Howard Hanson and the Rochester Phil-
harmonic Orchestra, Rochester, New York, May 1, 1925.
Dedicated to Harold Clurman

Symphony for Organ and Orchestra (1924)

> First performed by the New York Symphony Orchestra, Walter Damrosch conducting, with Nadia Boulanger as soloist, in New York City, January 11, 1925.
>
> Dedicated to Nadia Boulanger
>
> Boosey and Hawkes, Inc.

Grohg (1925), for Full Orchestra

> Ballet in one Act. Script by Harold Clurman.
>
> Unperformed.
>
> In Manuscript only

Music for the Theatre (1925), Suite for Small Orchestra

> 1. Prologue
> 2. Dance
> 3. Interlude
> 4. Burlesque
> 5. Epilogue
>
> First performed by Serge Koussevitzky and the Boston Symphony Orchestra in Boston, November 20, 1925.
>
> Dedicated to Serge Koussevitzky
>
> Boosey and Hawkes, Inc.
>
> Columbia Record

Dance Symphony (1925), Derived from the ballet "Grohg"

> First performed by Leopold Stokowski and the Philadelphia Orchestra, Academy of Music, Philadelphia, April 15, 1931.
>
> Dedicated to Harold Clurman
>
> Boosey and Hawkes, Inc.
>
> Victor Record

Concerto for Piano and Orchestra (1926)

> First performed by the Boston Symphony Orchestra, Koussevitzky conducting, with the composer at the piano, January 28, 1927.
>
> Dedicated to Alma Morgenthau

Boosey and Hawkes, Inc.

Columbia and Vanguard records

First Symphony (1928)

Orchestral version of "Symphony for Organ and Orchestra"

First performed by Ernest Ansermet and the Berlin Symphony Orchestra, Berlin, December, 1931.

Boosey and Hawkes, Inc.

Piano Variations (1930), Piano Solo

First performed by composer at a concert sponsored by League of Composers, Art Center, New York, January 4, 1931.

Dedicated to Gerald Sykes

Boosey and Hawkes, Inc.

Lyrichord, Concert Disc, Odyssey and Dover records

Short Symphony (No. 2) (1933)

First performed November 1934 by Orquésta Sinfónica de México under the direction of Carlos Chávez. First U.S. performance was a radio broadcast in 1944 by Leopold Stokowski and the NBC Symphony Orchestra.

Dedicated to Carlos Chávez

Boosey and Hawkes, Inc.

Statements (1934), for Symphony Orchestra

1. Militant
2. Cryptic
3. Dogmatic
4. Subjective
5. Jingo
6. Prophetic

Commissioned by the League of Composers for performance by Minneapolis Symphony Orchestra. First two movements performed by them under Eugene Ormandy, January 9, 1936.

Dedicated to Mary Senior Churchill

Boosey and Hawkes, Inc.

CBS Record

What Do We Plant? (1935), for Treble Voices and Piano

Written at request of Henry Street Music School in New York for performance by their girls' Glee Club

Boosey and Hawkes, Inc.

El Salón México (1936), for Symphony Orchestra

First performed by Orquésta Sinfónica de México, conducted by Carlos Chávez, August 27, 1937.

Arranged for Piano Solo and for Two Pianos, by Leonard Bernstein.

Boosey and Hawkes, Inc.

Westminster, Columbia, Mercury, Victor and Vanguard records

Two Children's Pieces (1936), Piano Solo

1. Sunday Afternoon Music
2. The Young Pioneers

Composed on invitation of Lazar Saminsky and Isadore Freed for inclusion in a collection of piano pieces for young people by contemporary composers. First performed by the composer in New York, February 24, 1936.

Fischer

Music for Radio (1937) (Saga of the Prairie), for Symphony Orchestra

Commissioned by Columbia Broadcasting System. First performed over CBS on July 27, 1937, by CBS Symphony Orchestra, Howard Barlow conducting.

Dedicated to Davidson Taylor

Boosey and Hawkes, Inc.

The Second Hurricane (1937), for Voices and Orchestra

A Play-Opera in two Acts for High School Performance

Libretto by Edwin Denby

Written at the request of Grace Spofford, Director of the

Music School of Henry Street Settlement, first performed
by them at the Playhouse in New York, April 21, 1937.
Staged by Orson Welles and conducted by Lehman Engel.
Dedicated to "Victor and Rudi and Germaine and Ruth, and
also Paul and Virgil"
Boosey and Hawkes, Inc.
Columbia Record

Billy the Kid (1938)
Ballet in one Act, choreography by Eugene Loring
Composed for Lincoln Kirstein's Ballet Caravan and first
produced in Chicago, October 1938.
Boosey and Hawkes, Inc.
Suite from the Ballet on Westminster, Columbia, Everest,
Mercury, Victor, Capitol records

An Outdoor Overture (1938), for High School Orchestra
Composed especially for the school orchestra of the High
School of Music and Art in New York City, where it was
first performed December 16, 1938, Alexander Richter
conducting.
Arranged for band by the composer.
Boosey and Hawkes, Inc.
Vanguard Record

Our Town (1940), for Orchestra
Music from the Film. Composed for Sol Lesser's film pro-
duction of Thornton Wilder's classic American Play "Our
Town." First performed by the Columbia Broadcasting
Orchestra conducted by Howard Barlow, June 9, 1940.
Boosey and Hawkes, Inc.
Vanguard Record

Sonata for Piano (1941)
First performed by the composer at a concert of La Nueva
Musica, Buenos Aires, October 21, 1941.
Dedicated to Clifford Odets, who commissioned it

Boosey and Hawkes, Inc.

Lyrichord, Epic and CRI records

Lincoln Portrait (1942), for Narrator and Orchestra

Commissioned by André Kostelanetz and first performed by him at Cincinnati, Ohio, May 14, 1942, with Cincinnati Symphony Orchestra. Text arranged by the composer from speeches and letters of Abraham Lincoln.

Dedicated to André Kostelanetz.

Arranged for Narrator and Band by Walter Beeler

Boosey and Hawkes, Inc.

Vanguard and Columbia records

Rodeo (1942)

Ballet in one Act, choreography by Agnes de Mille

Commissioned by the Ballet Russe de Monte Carlo, first presented at the Metropolitan Opera House, New York, October 16, 1942.

Boosey and Hawkes, Inc.

Four dance Episodes on Westminster, Columbia, Mercury, Victor and Capitol records

Sonata for Violin and Piano (1943)

First performed by Ruth Posselt and the composer at Town Hall, New York City, January 17, 1944.

Dedicated to Lt. Harry H. Dunham

Boosey and Hawkes, Inc.

Decca, CRI, and Allegro records

Appalachian Spring (1944)

Ballet in One Act. Script and choreography by Martha Graham. Commissioned for Martha Graham by the Elizabeth Sprague Coolidge Foundation. First performed as a ballet at Library of Congress, Washington, D.C., on October 30, 1944. Received the New York Music Critics Circle Award as the outstanding theatrical work of the season 1944–45.

Boosey and Hawkes, Inc.

Complete ballet on Columbia Record

Suite from ballet on Columbia, Victor, Mercury, Desto, Vanguard, Westminster and Everest records

Third Symphony (1946)

Commissioned by Koussevitzky Music Foundation. First performed on October 18, 1946, in Boston by Boston Symphony Orchestra under Serge Koussevitzky. Awarded the New York Music Critics Circle Award as the best orchestral work during the 1946–47 concert season.

Dedicated to the memory of Natalie Koussevitzky

Boosey and Hawkes, Inc.

Columbia, Everest and Mercury records

The Red Pony (1948)

Suite from music for the Film based on John Steinbeck's story. Picture produced and directed by Louis Milestone, New York premiere on March 8, 1949.

Dedicated to Erik Johns

Boosey and Hawkes, Inc.

Columbia and Decca records

Concerto for Clarinet and String Orchestra with Harp and Piano (1948)

Commissioned by Benny Goodman who premiered the concerto on November 6, 1950, with Fritz Reiner and the NBC Symphony Orchestra.

Dedicated to Benny Goodman

Reduced for Clarinet and Piano by the composer

Boosey and Hawkes, Inc.

Columbia Record

Old American Songs (1950, 1952), for Medium Voice and Piano

1. The Boatmen's Dance
2. The Dodger

3. Long Time Ago
4. Simple Gifts
5. I Bought Me a Cat
6. The Little Horses
7. Zion's Walls
8. The Golden Willow Tree
9. At the River
10. Ching-A-Ring Chaw
Boosey and Hawkes, Inc.
Columbia Record

The Tender Land (1954)
Opera in three Acts. Libretto by Horace Everett
Written on commission from Rodgers and Hammerstein for the thirtieth anniversary of the League of Composers. First performance April 1, 1954, by New York City Opera Company, Thomas Schippers, conductor.
Boosey and Hawkes, Inc.
Orchestral Suite from Opera (1957) on Victor Record
Down a Country Lane (1962), Arranged for School Orchestra
First published as a piece for piano in *Life Magazine* in its June 29, 1962, issue and written especially for young people studying music.
Boosey and Hawkes, Inc.
Music for a Great City (1964), for Symphony Orchestra
1. Skyline
2. Night Thoughts
3. Subway Jam
4. Toward the Bridge
Composed at the request of the London Symphony Orchestra. First performed by them at London's Festival Hall, May 26, 1964, composer as guest conductor.
Boosey and Hawkes, Inc.
CBS Record

Inscape (1967), for Symphony Orchestra
  Commissioned by the New York Philharmonic for its 125th
    Anniversary Year, premiered by them under the direction
    of Leonard Bernstein at the University of Michigan, Sep-
    tember 13, 1967.
  Boosey and Hawkes, Inc.

Bibliography

Aldrich, Richard, *Concert Life in New York 1902–1923*. New York: G. P. Putnam's Sons, 1941.

Antheil, George, *Bad Boy of Music*. Garden City: Doubleday, Doran & Company, Inc., 1945.

Beach, Sylvia, *Shakespeare and Company*. New York: Harcourt, Brace and Company, 1958.

Berger, Arthur, *Aaron Copland*. New York: Oxford University Press, 1953.

Copland, Aaron, *Copland on Music*. New York: Doubleday and Company, Inc., 1960.

  In paper: W. W. Norton & Company, Inc., 1963.

Music and Imagination. Cambridge: Harvard University Press, 1952.

  In paper: The New American Library (Mentor), 1959.

Our New Music. McGraw-Hill Book Company, Inc., 1941.

What to Listen For in Music. New York: McGraw-Hill Book Company, 1957.

  In paper: The New American Library (Mentor), 1964.

Clurman, Harold, *The Fervent Years*. New York: Alfred A. Knopf, Inc., 1950.

De Mille, Agnes, *Dance to the Piper*. Boston: Little, Brown and Company, 1952.

Erickson, Robert, *The Structure of Music*. New York: The Noonday Press, 1957 (paper).

Howard, John Tasker, *Our American Music*. New York: Thomas Y. Crowell Company, 1965.

Modern Music. New York: The New American Library (Mentor), 1958 (paper).

Imbs, Bravig, *Confessions of Another Young Man*. New York: Henkle-Yewdale House, Inc., 1936.

Machlis, Joseph, *The Enjoyment of Music*. New York: W. W. Norton & Company, Inc., 1963.

Norman, Gertrude and Shrifte, Miriam Lubell (Editors), *Letters of Composers, An Anthology 1603–1945*. New York: Alfred A. Knopf, Inc., 1946.

Rosenfeld, Paul, *Discoveries of a Music Critic*. New York: Harcourt, Brace and Company, 1936.

Sessions, Roger, *The Musical Experience of Composer, Performer, Listener*. Princeton: Princeton University Press, 1950.

Smith, Julia, *Aaron Copland*. New York: E. P. Dutton & Company, Inc., 1953.

Stearns, Marshall, *The Story of Jazz*. New York: Oxford University Press, 1956.

In paper: The New American Library (Mentor), 1958.

Thompson, Oscar, *Great Modern Composers*. New York: Dodd, Mead & Company, 1946.

Thomson, Virgil, *The Art of Judging Music*. New York: Alfred A. Knopf, Inc., 1948.

Index

CATHERINE OWENS PEARE writes for both children and adults, but more often for young readers. She began her writing career when she became editor of her high school paper. At New Jersey State Teachers College she was a frequent contributor to the campus literary quarterly. Professionally she has written over twenty-six books. Her biography of Mahatma Gandhi won a medal from the Boys Clubs of America, and her *Mark Twain* was a Junior Literary Guild selection. In 1962, she received the William Allen White and the Sequoyah awards for her biography, *The Helen Keller Story.*

Miss Peare bases her biographies on extensive research, and considers travel a vital part of the task. So far her subjects have taken her to thirteen foreign countries and to many parts of the United States. "Any story, fiction or nonfiction, has a truer ring if the author was *there*," she says. Catherine Owens Peare lived for many years in Brooklyn, New York, and now resides in Connecticut.

MIRCEA VASILIU was born in Bucharest, Rumania. He became a published author at thirteen with a book about school life, illustrated by the author, but was trained at the University of Bucharest for a diplomatic career. He found time to study art later at the Corcoran School in Washington, D.C., where he served in Rumania's diplomatic corps. When Rumania was drawn into the Communist circle, Mr. Vasiliu was granted asylum in the United States. In his new life he turned his longtime hobby of drawing into a career. He has illustrated many books, notably some of Emily Kimbrough's, and is author-illustrator of several children's books and two autobiographies. He and his wife live in New York.

ABOUT THE BOOK: The text is set in Caledonia; display type is Caslon Old Face italic; and the book was printed by offset. Mircea Vasiliu's drawings are executed in pen and ink with wash, for a light and free effect.